ZEN
AND THE INFLECTION OF THE REFLECTION

FURTHER ZEN RAMBLINGS FROM THE INTERNET

SCOTT SHAW

BUDDHA ROSE PUBLICATIONS

Zen and the Inflection of the Reflection
Copyright © 2022 by Scott Shaw
www.scottshaw.com
ALL RIGHTS RESERVED

Cover Photographs by Scott Shaw
Copyright © 2022—All Rights Reserved

Rear Cover Photograph of Scott Shaw
by Hae Won Shin
Copyright © 2022—All Rights Reserved

First Edition 2022

This book contains material protected under International and Federal Copyright Laws and Treaties. Any unauthorized reprint or use of this material is prohibited. No part of this book may be reproduced or transmitted in any form or by any means, electronic or mechanical, including photocopying, recording, or by any information storage and retrieval system without express written permission from the author or publisher.

ISBN 10: 1-949251-47-0
ISBN 13: 978-1-949251-47-0

Library of Congress Control Number: 2022934579

10 9 8 7 6 5 4 3 2 1
Printed in the United States of America

ZEN
AND THE INFLECTION OF THE REFLECTION

Introduction

Here it is, *The Scott Shaw Zen Blog 22.0,* originally presented on the *World Wide Web.* All of the writings presented in this book were written between November of 2021 and March of 2022.

As was the case with the previously published volumes based upon *The Scott Shaw Zen Blog;* entitled: *Scribbles on the Restroom Wall, The Chronicles: Zen Ramblings from the Internet, Words in the Wind, Zen Mind Life Thoughts, The Zen of Life, Lies and Aberrant Reality, Apostrophe Zen, The Abstract Arsenal of Zen and the Psychology of Being, Zen and Again: The Metaphysical Philosophy of Psychology, Tempest in a Teapot and the Den of Zen, Buddha in the Looking Glass, Wo Ton' of the Blue Vision, Zen and the Psychology of the Spiritual Something, Pyrophoric Zen, Fragments of Paradox, Zen: Traversing the Entity of Non-Entity, Zen and the Ambient Echo: The Psychological Philosophy of Being, Paritical Zen and the Life Science of Becoming No Thing, Obscurist Occulto: Hiding from the Definition of Meaning, Principles of the Precepts, Left Turn at Reality Central, Zen and the Outside of the Inside,* and *Garage Sale Zen* this volume is presented exactly as it was viewed on *scottshaw.com* with no rewriting, punctuation, or typo corrections. From this, we hope you will receive the original reading experience.

This volume of internet ramblings is presented with the date and time listed as to when each blog was originally posted. Also, the blogs in this volume are presented from last to first. With this, we hope to present a transcendence back through time as opposed to an evolving evolution. In addition, we left out the traditional *Table of Contents* in an attempt to leave this volume with a much more free-flowing reading experience.

Okay, there's the information and the definitions. Read on… We hope you enjoy it. And, be sure to stayed tuned for the ongoing *Scott Shaw Zen Blog* @ *scottshaw.com*.

How Zen is Your Zen?
01/Mar/2022 08:47 AM

What are you thinking about right now? No really, what are you thinking about right now? Do you ever think about what you are thinking about? Do you ever study your thoughts? Do you ever study, (look deep down inside of yourself), and question why you are thinking what you are thinking? If you do, that is great because you would be one of the very few who does.

How much control do you possess over what you think? Yes, everybody sees and embraces the world with a sense defined by who they have been cast to be. But, why do you—why are you locked into the pattern of thought that you are locked into? And, more importantly, why do you have little or no control over your thoughts?

The fact of life is, people are trained to simply embrace their thoughts with whatever sense of urgency they may hold. This urgency is defined by what emotions they hold towards the whatever of the whatever that is being ushered into their life. When they are emotional, they truly feel. When they are not emotional, their life is left to an abyss of looking for something to feel something about. As long as they can keep their mind focused on the reaching for fantasy, they do not have to study who and what they truly are and/or who and what their thoughts, their words, their actions does to the anyone else and the world outside of themselves. In other words, the world of thought is generally a very selfish sphere of reality.

Think how much is going on in everyone's mind all across the globe. Think how many people are praying right now for guidance, for help, for getting what they want. How about you? Again, what are you thinking about right now?

Most people lose themselves in the desire of desire and find they are only happily thinking when their desires are being met—when they are in control, and when all things are the way they want them to be. Think about your own life, when are you happy? Mostly likely, you are happy when you are getting what you want. Thus, that emotion fills your thoughts.

Turn this around, and when are you unhappy? Mostly likely, it is when you are not getting what you want.

The thing is, most people allow these two elemental emotions to dominate their entire life and define how they feel and what they are thinking about. The problem is, if you live your life defined in this manner, there is only one primarily focus; yourself. Even if you state, in your own mind, that you are thinking about someone else, that someone else is only in your mind because they fulfill that something that you want. Thus, they are in your thoughts. Or, they are in your thoughts because you are angry with them because they are not giving you what you want.

If you step back and realize the truth in this, then you will conclude that you are not in control of your thoughts and/or your emotions at all. You are completely controlled by what the Out There is proving or keeping from you. Truly, is that the best way you should be living your life?

If you want to know Self Truth, there is only one way to do it. If you hope to find Enlightenment, Self-Actualization, Self-Awareness, by whatever name you wish to call it, or to simply live a good and refined life, then you need to take hold of your mind and shift it from being controlled by all the Out There.

Can you do it? I don't know, can you? Some people have. Those are the people who have left a loving imprint onto the world stage. Is that going to be you or are you simply going to be controlled by thoughts, driven by emotions, that you possess no true control over?

How Zen is your Zen?

People You Don't Want to Know
28/Feb/2022 01:32 PM

    I think for each of us, there are times in our life when we are forced to interact with and deal with somebody we really don't like—someone that we wish was not in our life. I guess for some people, they love everyone. But, I don't know??? That just doesn't seem all that doable.

    I know for me, there are people who try to come into my life all the time. They do it for all kinds of reason, I guess? And though, I always try to be nice to everyone and treat everyone with respect, the fact of the fact is, a lot of these people I just do not want to know.

    Like I have long stated, *"Everybody wants something from me, but nobody ever gives me anything."* And, that has really remained the case for much of my life. How about you? Are you one of those people that other people want things from or are you one of those people who wants things from someone else. It's really the Yin and Yang. There really doesn't seem to be an in-between ground.

    I get it, it's my own fault. Ever since I got into the writing game, the music game, the film game, the etc..., it puts me in a position of having a bullseye on my life. Some people love me, some people hate me, some people want to be my friend, some people wish to hurt me. Some people want what I own so they don't have to work for it themselves and they try to take it from me. But, why? Why must people forever reach outside of themselves? Why must people want something from someone else? Why can't they be a self-contained combat unit like Don Jackson and I used to always jokingly describe ourselves.

    You know, I find it very curious that many people come at you with a smile on their face and an extended hand of friendship. But, when you don't give them what they want, (whatever that may be), they turn to insults and threats. Not cool!

I think we have to take a deeper look at this. I believe we need to question the motivations of others based upon our own motivations for reaching out and into the life of someone else.

Think about a time when you reached out to someone that you did not know. What was you reason for doing so? There was a reason. You reached out to them wanting something. Be honest with yourself. What was it?

Maybe it was friendship. Maybe it was lust. Maybe you wanted something they had. Truly, what was it?

Of course, each separate case is defined individually by its own set of circumstances. But, I believe there is probably one common element. If you are honest with yourself, you wanted something they have or you wanted something they could give you.

Now, ask yourself, if your initial communication is not met with a commonality of reciprocation, how do you feel—how do you behave? How does your feelings about that other person change?

If you are a true person, those feelings don't change at all. But, if you are locked into a space of want or wanting something, then you are probably left with feelings of at least mild animosity. Perhaps your acrimony is much larger than that. But, why should you feel that way? Is feeling that a good feeling? Is feeling that way the other person's fault? No. Isn't it simply your frustration with you not getting what you desired?

In the perfect world, all people would simply embrace a conscience interactive common reality. But, there is desire in play. And, most people cannot and will not truly frame the reality of their life in a manner that is clearly understood and defined. This is because of the fact they do not possess an honest appraisal of what they truly want from a person and do not take control over how they will act if they do not receive it. In other words, they lie to themselves and they lie to others.

So, here's the thing, *"Don't be that person."* Don't be the person who pursuits someone just so you can get something. If you want to reach out a hand of friendship based in purity, truth, and mutual admiration, do so. If things work out and you become friends; great! If you get what you hoped for; excellent! But, if a person really does not want to know you or interact with you, have the respect for human life and do not force your way into their life; trying to take what is thier's only to satisfy your own ego, greed, and wanting's.

    Be honest with yourself about who you truly are and what you truly want. Be honest with others about why you wish to become a fixture in their life. Mostly, never force your way into a person's life. If they don't want you to be a part of their life, be honest and whole enough to stay out of their life.

Right Now
27/Feb/2022 01:17 PM

Do you remember the Van Halen song, *"Right Now?"* Though in the video for the song there is a few humorous suggestions made, the idea of the song is very powerful. Right Now what are you thinking about? Right Now what are you doing? Right Now what are you going to do next?

Right Now, Russia is invading the Ukraine. That is just wrong! There are a lot of people who are feeling the pain for those people, and some even wish they could go there and join the fight. Though I am not even going to go into the fact of how many times, throughout history, one nation has invaded another but what I will say, Right Now, what are you planning to do next?

All life, all attacks, all invasions, all wars, boil down to one individual hurting another. This scale can become grand, as in the case of Ukraine, but it began by one person taking one action and then setting an entire course of events into motion. Again, Right Now, what are you going to do? Is what you are going to do going to hurt someone and set a negative course of events into motion in their life? Or, is what you are going to do going to make something very good happen that saves one person and possibly more from pain?

Throughout history there have been wars. Throughout history there have been attacks. Throughout history there have been fights. But, all of this evil begin by one person in their Right Now doing something that hurts someone else. It does not have to be that way. The choice in the Right Now can be made to do good, to forgive, to help, and to do nothing harmful or hurtful.

You do have a choice in life. What are you going to do with your Right Now? Are you going to hurt someone? Are you going to set a course of events into motion that will cause someone pain? Or, are you going to do something that will help someone? Are you going to do something that will set a course of events into motion that will help all humanity?

Right Now, are you going to sit there, pretending nothing is going on and that there is nothing that you can do? Or, Right Now are you going to get up, get motivated, and help one person or a million people. This is your Right Now. What are you going to do with it?

So Woke They'll Never Get Sleepy
27/Feb/2022 07:18 AM

I watched the William Friedkin documentary the other night. He is one of those incredible directions who has created some very important pieces of cinema. It was an interesting documentary. Friedkin looks so great for his age!

During the doc, they discussed a lot of his movies. One of the features they focused on was, *Cruising,* starring Al Pacino. Tarantino did a bit on it. I wonder why they never ask me to be in one of those documentaries?

Anyway, Tarantino, he spoke about how hard core many of the movies of that era were. And, it's true. You just can no longer present on the screens of the A-Market the style of cinema that was shown in the '60s, '70s, or like *Cruising,* in 1980.

I originally saw *Cruising* in the theatre back when it was first released. I imagine I've seen little pieces of it here or there over the years when it was on Broadcast TV, but, being reminded of it, and with nothing better to watch, I pulled it up, On-Demand, and rewatched it.

Viewing it, it was one of those films that I realized I did not remember very much about. You know how it is, some movies you remember every moment, but other ones leave your mind over time. So, it was like seeing it for the first time. And yes, like Tarantino said, there was a lot of very explicit stuff going on in that film. But, it is a very good movie.

You know, I've watched the world change a lot over the years I've been alive. ...Sixty-three years at this moment of my life. I've witnessed the sixties and into the seventies when everything was becoming freer and I've seen the eighties, with things like AIDS, where everything became more and more shut down. Even in me, as the years have progressed, I see how what I would have done back then, I would no longer do. This being said, it seems society, our society, has become more and more shut down but not necessarily in a good way. It seems that now everyone is so quick to throw accusations about the badness of that someone else. Blaming them for their own personal life dilemma. It seems that people want to use this blame as a means for taking from that someone else or getting what they were never promised. It's kind of strange really. Once upon a time, it was all about taking personal responsibility, now it is so much more about casting the blame and making that someone else culpable for something that YOU claim you had no role in creating or instigating.

I believe something is really lost in all of this. I mean, it is easy to hurl blame. It is easy to believe that you are right and they are wrong. It is even easy to use this a method to try to get what you want from either that someone or from the greater whole of reality but what is lost in all of this is the YOU in the creation. What is your responsibility in creating your own anything?

So often I see people wanting something from someone else; whatever that something may be. But, why don't they just go and create it themselves? Why can't they? Why do they want to take from someone else? Then, when and if they don't get given that gift that they want, they get mad—they cast blame. But, who's fault is it? Theirs for wanting something and not being able to create it themselves or the person who does not or cannot not give them what they crave?

This all plays into the reality of the reality of the time we find ourselves in. Once upon time, people took pride in being self-strong and creating their own reality—whatever that reality may be. Now, it seems it is so much easier to focus outside of the self and want what that other person is not willing to give. And, when they don't give it or, when they do that something that YOU do not like, they are, *"Canceled."*

I don't know? What was done then, was done then. It was a different era. Freer, yes. Is freer better? Probably. Now, it seems it is all about the take and the blame.

When we look around at our current reality, all there seems to be is a lot of, *"Don't."* There is a lot of what you're not supposed to do. And, if you do it, you are wrong and bad and no good. But, who is the ultimate judge of any of that? Once upon a time, it was okay. Now???

So, I think we all need to look at ourselves. Moreover, I think we all need to stop looking outside of ourselves. We especially need to re-realize that we are the creative force of not only our life but all of the reality around us.

Stop wanting anything from anyone else. Stop taking. Stop judging. Let everyone be as they want to be while you strive to be the best, most creative, most perfect representation of life that you can become. Focus on making YOU the best YOU that YOU can be and not taking, not judging, not demeaning anyone in the world around you, not matter what you logic or reasoning. Because trust me, what you are doing today will, most likely, be criticized and looked down on tomorrow. Then where will you be?

Take the Karma; Please!
26/Feb/2022 07:22 AM

If you are a guitar player, you may understand what I'm about to say. Whenever I pick up a used or vintage guitar and start to play it, somehow the vibes of that guitar overtakes my playing style. For example, maybe I will pick up a guitar and, all of a sudden, I find myself playing the blues. Though I, of course, appreciate the blues, it is not the style I normally play. Yet, there I am doing blues notes. I don't know, I'm very sensitive to that sort of thing.

I've always believed that the reason this happens is that the person who owned the guitar previously put all kinds of their energy into that instrument and, because of this fact, that playing energy lingers and will influence the next player. Of course, over time, if I buy the guitar or something, then the energy changes. It changes to my playing style. But, it just feels that instruments hold an energy. If musical instruments can do this, why wouldn't all other aspects of life?

Most of life goes by in a blur and people never really look into the subtle energy of things, places, and people. Certainly, when you go into specific places, they hold a very specific energy. There are churches that hold a very strong energy. There are geographic land locations that are very powerful and so on. You go there, you feel it.

People also hold and project a very specific energy. I believe that it is very easy to take note of the energy of a person when they are one of those sorts that is rude, loud, or aggressive. But, most people are not that overt. Yet, they each possess a specific energy that they expel to the world.

For example, I eat in restaurants a lot so over the many decades of my life I have come to know many a food worker. Recently, I have encounter two young female servers who are both so good at their job it is almost scary. In one of these instances, this new girl started working at a restaurant I frequent that has this very complicated rewards system. I have witnessed the other servers and even the manager not know how to access it. This girl was there for like a week and she was a master of it. More than that, I watch her, and she is doing everyone else's job. She runs around taking care of so many customers and doing so many things for the other servers and hosts and etc., that it is not even funny.

In another case, there is this restaurant that I have been going to for decades. They currently have this server that is literally the best worker who has ever been there. I mean, she runs around! She is really good! I told her so yesterday. I told her that she is the best worker we have ever had there. She was just dumbfounded and so thankful for the compliment. But, she deserved it! Whereas most people just project an energy of doing what they have to do to get by and get the job done, these two people are driven.

There is this certain part of me that questions, why if they are so good at their job, can't they move forward into something bigger and better? There is certainly nothing wrong with being a restaurant worker. Like I said, I go to them all the time. But, it just seems that these two young woman could have a greater destiny.

Like I wrote in one of the first blog I created. It's actually on this blog, down near the bottom, as it was one of the Greatest Hits, *Trapped by Circumstance.* Anyway, it seems that sometimes people are just locked into a destiny that they cannot escape. Though they have the potential for greatness in life, but life reality keeps them bound. They have the drive, the desire, and the projection of energy to rise above but, due to their life circumstance, they cannot.

Again, we get back to this truth of energy. You are an encapsulated individual. You are unique entity. You are a projection of your energy. But, what energy are you going to project? And, the energy that you project sets a whole world of life, life attributes, and life compilations into motion.

What you do with the energy you project not only affects you but it affects everyone else it affects.

For example, I've recently been reminded of the fact that my *Zen Filmmaking* brother, Donald G. Jackson, cast a lot of energy onto my life. Even in his death, I am forced to deal with it.

When he was literally on his deathbed at U.C.L.A., he wanted to make sure that I would keep his filmmaking legacy alive, as he believed he could trust no one else. I happily said yes. He also asked me to do all I could to bury and hopefully have one of his films forgotten. I agreed.

You see, the fact is, Don had a deep religious rebirth in the later few years of his life. Though he was obviously a very flawed individual, you cannot deny his beliefs. From this, he truly hated the fact that there was blatant female abuse in that one film. Me too. I hate that kind of stuff in movies! So, I agreed.

He passed away before the digital age truly hit, where anyone can and will do anything online and let the creator be damned. A few people released the movie without the rights to do so, but it was eventually removed from sales. But, for the most part, the film faded away as he had wished. Every now and then I get hit up by some fan of his works who wants to release it. But, they just don't understand Don's truth or his motivations. Then, when I tell them the story, they get mad at me. Some have even threaten me. First of all, Take the Karma; Please! Do you think I want to be the one left trying to protect and keep hidden a film that projects such negativity and have people attack me because of it? No, I do not. I feel like the husband and wife team in those *Annabelle* movies. Trying to hide away the doll's evil energy. But, I made a promise to a dying man. A dying man who had re-found his god and wanted to make amends. Yet, he created an energy with that film. That film and a few others he created projects a certain negative energy. So, what can be done?

This is the thing with life and with life energy that you really need to take into consideration. People do what they do. They either do it from a position of hard work and goodness, like I spoke about with those two young women. Or, they do things that project a darkness. The thing is, some people like that darkness. They like to see people hurt. Sure, it's just a movie and not real life but all things that are done are projected and they are sent out to the world while expressing an energy. This is why it is so important that you truly study the energy that you are directing to the world and how what you do/what you create expands outwards to the rest of humanity. Energy is palpable. Energy is dispersible. Energy projects. If you do something that is negative, if you embrace things that are negative, that energy spreads outward from you to the world. This is the same if you do something positive.

You can be that worker who does the best job possible, no matter what your job is—spreading goodness to all those you interact with. Or, you can be the person who invokes and/or embraces negativity. Which energy do you want to project? Which energy do you want to disperse onto that guitar that you are playing that will influence the next person who plays it?

The Intention of Your Intention
25/Feb/2022 07:27 AM

Yesterday, I spoke about the Buddhist understanding of, *"Cetanā," "Intention."* …How your intention is what sets all of the cause and all of the effect into motion in your life. …How your intention not only affects all that you are to become but also how it affects everyone else your intention impacts. I believe we need to take a deeper look into this subject to provide a more enhanced understanding.

The thing is, and perhaps this is the most complicated concept in truly understanding the path of true intention, is that most people believe whatever it is they are doing is right. They think what they are doing is for the betterment of themselves and maybe even the better of all. The problem is, anything motivated by Unrefined Self has the potential to do more damage than good. As is commonly understood in Buddhism, if you hurt anyone, you hurt everyone and, thus, all of your actions can be seen as wrong and negative.

For a very large example of this, and something that is taking place right now, we can view the invasion of Ukraine instigated by Russian President Vladimir Putin. If you understand the history of Russia, you know that Ukraine and the capital of Ukraine, Kyiv, played an essential role in Russia's historic development. This is at least a stated part of Putin's claim as a reason for his invasion. Though most people of the world see this invasion as a travesty, in the mind of Putin, he has his intention. And, he believes his intention to be just and right.

Of course, most people never possess the power of someone like Vladimir Putin to be able to unleash this level of carnage, but each person believes what they are doing they are doing for a just and right reason. This is why so many people unleash damage to the life of other people and create ongoing negative events in their own life. …What they did, they did for a reason, a reason that was very logical in their own mind, but as that reason was self-motivated, what they did set about a course of negative events in the life of someone else and, thus, that negativity came back to haunt the original doer.

Think about all of the business dealings that go on out there all the time. All of these people are doing all of these things attempting to create more money and a better life for themselves. What they are doing, they probably believe is right, but what they are doing is hurting someone else.

Think about all of the broken hearts out there. Someone loves somebody else, so they pursue that person. They believe if they could only be with that person, all things would be right with their world, the world of that other person, and the whole world in general. But, the other person doesn't feel the same way about them and thus they do not follow the path of the relationship the one induvial wanted. Thus, a person's heart is broken. Both people possess their objectives. Both people had their intent. But, their intent equaled heartbreak. Who was at fault?

This is the thing about intent and the reason so many people's lives are hurt by their own intent and the intent of others; one person's intent is not the same as anyone else's. What one person feels—what one person believes to be right, is not what another person feels is true.

Okay… That's the facts… Then, what is the proper way to interact with your intent and to encounter your life so as not to cast negativity, based on your intent, onto others? The simple answer is, *"Don't."* Don't do simply because you can do. Don't act out simply because you can act out. Don't take simply because you can take. Don't force someone to do anything simply because you have the power to force them. Don't overpower simply because you can overpower. Don't cast your judgment simply because you can cast your judgment. Don't believe you know what is right for someone else. And mostly, don't hurt if you know what you are about to do is going to hurt anyone or anybody.

No one ever said life was easy, just, or fair. But, the reason it is not easy, just, or fair is because people believe that their (that your) intention should be universally embraced. But, should it? Just because you want something, does that mean that you deserve that something? Just because you believe you are right, does not actually make you right? No. It simply means that you possess a certain belief. But, you must embrace the fact, if you hope to live a good and conscious life, that what you believe may not be believed by that someone else you are attempting to involve in the pursuit of your intention.

Intention is a powerful life tool. But, it is misused by most people. All you have to do is to look around at the world, look around at life, look around at the people who have used their intention and their intension has negatively affected the life of someone else. Where did they eventually end up? What was the final definition of their life? Were they universally loved? Or, were they despised?

If you hurt one person, you hurt everyone. Keep that in mind. If you are only thinking about yourself, if your are only acting on your own intention, and believing what you want is right, you are only thinking about yourself. Study your intention. Know why you possess any intention. Never invoke your intention if it has the potential to hurt anyone. You want to live a good and spiritual life, that is the key.

The Cost of Your Karma
24/Feb/2022 07:10 AM

Recently, I've been writing a lot about human personal interaction and the way it affects the condition of a person's life. Because really, isn't that all we have? Our life. What we live. How we live. And, who comes into our life.

Each person brings with them a certain set of lived reality. For some, that reality is defined by goodness, caring, and the desire to help. For others, that reality is desired by wanting. In either case, who we meet and what they do once we meet them comes to not only affect our life, the choices we are presented with, but ultimately what we do with what that other person has brought into our life.

We all know the various types of people. There are those who want to give us something and those who want to take something from us. Of course, most life interactions are not that cut and dry as most people exist somewhere in between these two extremes. But, no matter the cause or the case, what a person first desires and then chooses to do is what sets the entire rest of their life into motion and it directly affects all those who are affected by their desires and their choices.

Throughout history, this is why some people have chosen to retreat to places like monasteries. It is believed that the farther you remove yourself from the world, the less internal conflict you will encounter. Of course, this is true. This is why many people retreat to whatever safe hiding place they can find. The less you do, the fewer people you interact with, the number of your life problem substantially diminishes.

Over the past couple of decades, life and life interaction has changed drastically due to the development of the internet. People live, work, buy, sell, and interact on a scale that was impossible just a few years ago. For some, they find this appealing. For others, however, all kinds of life interaction comes at them in ways they never imagined that they do not want or appreciate. Today, the fact is, virtually no one is not affected by this human construct that has taken on its own identity in many ways. It has become virtually impossible to retreat. From this, the pathway of human existence has drastically been altered. One may argue that this factor has not changed the true personality of a person. Though this may be true, it has given everyone a new set of tools to live their life by if they wish to partake of them.

From this and because of this, what a person chooses to do with their life has the potential to affect others in not only so many previously unknown ways but also to direct a person's life down an either positive or negative pathway.

This is where life gets complicated. This is where life has always gotten complicated. What are you going to do with the tools at your disposal? Are you going to use them to get what you want? Are you going to use them to give someone else what they want? Are you going to use them to fulfill your own desires? Or, are you going to employee them to give to someone and/or remove the hurt from someone else's life? Are you going to help or are your going to hurt?

Most people do not take the time to truly understand why they are doing what they are doing and what effect it will have on that someone else that they might not even know. But, hurt anyone and everyone is hurt. One hurt has the potential to move from your single action and go on to hurt a multitude of other people. This is also the case if you help one person. This positive action has the potential to move outwards and create a great world of giving.

But, why are you doing what you are doing? This is a question few people as themselves. Few people ask themselves this question because they do not want to know the answer. They may possess a million rationalizations. And, even if they believe what they are doing is being done for someone else, it is them who is instigating the desire to do what they are doing. Thus, the truth be told, all they are doing is doing something for themselves. Some people are fine with this fact. But, if they are, (if you are), then what does that say about that person. It says, they do not care about anybody but themselves and all they are doing is being done with only themselves and their own set of wants and desires in their mind. How can that be a good thing?

In Buddhism, it is understood that all life actions are defined by the Sanskrit word, *"Cetanā."* This word means, *"Intention."* Your intention is what sets your actions into motion and your intention is what will ultimatly defines what your actions will equal—not only to your life but to the life of all those affected by what you choose to do.

In the Satipatthana Sutta the condition known as, *"Mindfulness,"* or, *"Sati,"* in Sanskrit is explained. It details how one can consciously encounter life. But, you don't have to read a sutra to understand what is right or wrong and how you can behave in a conscious manner in your life. You simply must be willing to view the possible consequences of your actions on a grander scale than simply how what you are going to do will affect you. You must reach outwards from self-consciousness to view the grand scale of all humanity and see how what you do will affect that next one person and may spread outwards to affect numerous others.

Doing right is always a very obvious choice. Justifying your doing something that will hurt someone/anyone else is always the wrong choice. It's really very simply. That is mindfulness. Caring enough to choose not to hurt the life of anyone but to put whatever desire you have away and help.

What you do with your life is your choice. But, as in all things life, there will always be consequences, both good and bad. If you help, you have helped. That will spread outwards. If you hurt, you have hurt. That too will spread outwards. Whether you help or hurt one person or millions, that will come to be the definition of your life and will either cost your life a lot or you will be rewarded in goodness.

Ask yourself these simple questions before you do anything, *"Is what I am about to do going to make me smile? Is what I am about to do going to make the person I am doing it to smile?"* Your answer will tell you what you should or should not do.

Your life is your choice. But know, for everything you do, there will always be a price to pay. If not today, someday.

Choose mindfulness over desire. Choose to care more about that someone else than yourself. That is true enlightenment.

Roller Blade Seven: The Never-Ending Story
23/Feb/2022 05:13 PM

As I say way too often, *"It doesn't seem like a week ever goes by when I am not asked some question about The Roller Blade Seven, am insulted as per it's creation, or someone gives me some nonsense about something involving RB7."* I certainly never expected that when Don Jackson and I were creating the movie. And, to be truthful, I really don't want it now. Why it has held whatever place it has in the Cult Film Hierarchy, is beyond me. When I started out on the film, I thought we were going to make an action-adventure flick. Wrong! I would have far preferred that it would have just been forgotten and maybe when I'm ninety years old someone found it on some old video tape as they were tracking through the elements of history and then came and interviewed me, asking, *"WTF?"*

Roller Blade Seven was distributed across the globe. It has been set in many languages. And, as I have written in numerous places, I never got any of that money. And it made a lot of money. I'm not going to go into the whole Hollywood world of rip offs here, and who did what and why, but I will state an interesting point, (and I have also mentioned this fact in some of the pieces I have written about my interaction with the creation of this film in the past), I never signed any release(s) for the rights to any of my creative contributions. In fact, nor did the publishers of my books because they would have had to release their rights, as well. Thus, no one and no company who ever distributed the film had the right to do so; at least not in using my image, my music, the words from my books that make up much of the dialogue of the film, and all the other etc. I did. Thus, they all were guilty of copyright infringement. The fact is, I was promised to be paid, I never was. Moreover, it was sold to so many countries and changed hands through various distributors, who could I sue? Plus, all that's very expensive and, as I've talked about in the past, when we finished the film, I had worked for free, and with getting none of the back-end money I was promised, I was dead broke.

Now, this all may sound like a, *"Woe is me,"* piece, but it is not. It's just putting some facts out there. It's just stating some facts about the Hollywood Game. I mean, here I am, thirty years later—thirty years after the creation of that film, and some people still use it as a definition of me. But, is it? Was it ever? No. Plus, DGJ passed-away long ago, so I am the only one they seek out.

And, the fact is, I have made so many other films that were better representations of my creative vision, but few people speak to me about those. They want to talk about a bad movie and its sequel and somehow use those features as the definition of my life.

I am under no illusion about what *The Roller Blade Seven* and *Return of the Roller Blade Seven* actually are. You're not going to get an argument from me about how bad they are. The only difference is, I was there. I was one of the two creative forces that produced those pieces of *Zen Cinema*. So, for me, it's all an inside joke as I was there all the way through; from begin, to end, to today.

I believe this is something you really need to think about as you cast your definitions onto other people. The fact of the fact is, if you weren't there, you cannot know the inside truth. You don't know the true truth about the person. You don't know the true truth about the how and the why and the what happened because of the what happened. So, who are you to think anything about anybody? Don't you think it's just better to focus on your own development and not to lose yourself in apprising the life and becoming obsessed about what someone else has created? Because, the fact of the fact is, you can never truly understand someone else's reason why.

For those of you who want to check out this bizarre piece of *Zen Filmmaking* history, you can view it on YouTube. I put it up there a while back. Enjoy ☺

* * *
23/Feb/2022 09:39 AM

If you're always looking for reason to be angry at something you can always find one.

But, does that make your life any better?

Does that make anyone's life any better?

Forgive and look beyond the limitations.

*   *   *
23/Feb/2022 08:54 AM

What are you planning to do today?

Are you thinking only about yourself or are your going to do something to help someone else have a better, happier, and more fulfilled life?

Personal Crisis
23/Feb/2022 07:40 AM

  The world is going on all around us. There is all this stuff taken place all over the globe. Some of it is really intense, some it may be very beautiful, everybody is living what they are living but what are you living?
  Your life may be going along fine but then someone or something steps in and really messes things up. Though all this other stuff, (much bigger and more important stuff), is going on all around you, though everything was fine just a minute ago, now all you can think about is that one thing that someone exposed your life to.
  I think we've all experienced situations like this. Somebody brings something new into your life and you just don't want it there—you just don't want to deal with it. It doesn't make your life any better. But, it certainly makes everything, if not worse, at least more complicated.
  I think we all try to avoid these situations. I know I do. Just let the world go on and don't bring your melodrama into my sphere of existence, that's my moto. But, it seems sometimes you just can't keep it away.
  Some people can just tune this stuff out. Somebody sucker punches them and they just do not even care. That's great if you can do that. Most of us aren't like that, I don't think.
  I know some people like to create controversy in the life of those around them. I really don't know why they do this? I guess it gives them some sense of power. Others, just want to control all that is not theirs. They reach out into the lives that they had nothing to do with creating—they reach into other people's life space just to turn it upside down. I always question why can't a person just live their own life and not try to infiltrate the life, the possessions, the duties, and the doings of someone else? I guess, some just want to

take control over or take away what someone else was given. Why is again anyone's guess?

As we all know, these things are going to probably happen, though we certainly wish they would not. But, what can we do about that? What do you do? I don't really have an answer as lord knows I was never a highly functioning sociopath who thinks only about myself. I try to always take the well-being of the other person into consideration before I do anything. When that kind of stuff comes my direction I just try to rationalize it, steer clear from people like that, and let the cards fall where they may, and then accept the outcome as best as I can. Sometimes that works, sometimes it does not. Again, how about you? What do you do?

I think the big problem in all of this is how it takes over your thought process. You are left thinking about something you do not wish to be thinking about.

I also believe we need to look at the people who bring this style of life experience into play. Why are they doing it? The most common answer is that they want something from you. They want something: be that some possession, your money, your love, your sex, your honor, some something. You have it, they want it, so they create controversy in your life. They may ask for it, they may threaten you for it, they may simply steal it. But, the source point is they want that something. And, in some cases, that something they want, is simply to take your peace away from you and make you upset and/or make you hurt.

I think we all know, that taking something from someone is wrong. I think we all know that hurting someone is wrong. We all should know that creating situations of controversy in someone's life should also be incorrect. But, it goes on all around us all the time. All based in the demented personal empowerment of some person. The problem is, when someone brings that something your direction, it is only you left dealing with the aftermath.

I suppose there is no one true answer to this. I suppose there is not one solution. The only thing I believe can be done, to mitigate as much damage as possible, is for you to not take part in the confrontation. Don't get sucked into what that someone else is attempting to create.

I wish people did not try to take things from other people. I wish people did not try to steal someone else's peace. But, most people only care about themselves, they only care about what they can get for themselves. The only solution, if there is one at all, is don't give them the benefit of your caring. They may take from you, they may try to mess up your life, but if you do not care, what have the won. And, as I have seen time-and-time-and-time again in life is that, the people who do this kind of stuff are the ones who ultimately end up experiencing the pain. What you sow so shall you reap.

"Do not be deceived: God cannot be mocked. A man reaps what he sows. The one who sows to please his sinful nature, from that nature will reap destruction; the one who sows to please the Spirit, from the Spirit will reap eternal life." Epistle to the Galatians, 6:7

Finding God
22/Feb/2022 07:46 AM

I forever find it very interesting how when a person is nearing the end of their life they become very religious. I guess it is natural as for one to walk through that final door takes a lot of stamina. This is especially the case when a person has become more and more ill over time and they know the end is coming soon.

The thing is, though people seemingly become more religious as their death is approaching, maybe they even pray that they can find redemption, that means that the religion was in them all of the time. They simply did not choose to embrace it.

As a child, most of us are indoctrinated into religion. We are taken to church, we are taught to pray, we are told we should be a good individual or god will punish us. Thus, with all of this programming, there is almost no way that we cannot have religion in our brains from the time we are children forward.

I imagine we have all known people who have done bad things to other people. Often times this is based in them getting money or gaining power over someone for some reason. Where was the god in them at that point? Where was their religion? Yet, when they are coming close to their death, they pray and they pray and hope for forgiveness so they can enter the kingdom of heaven.

Let's make this a little bit more personal… Think about something you have done that you did to get money when it was not rightfully yours or something that you did that hurt or infringed on the life of someone else. If you haven't done anything like that, good for you! But, if you have, even if it was a small thing, truly bring it to mind.

I think we all understand why people do things to get money. …We all need to survive. But, when someone takes something from someone else, to get that money, what kind of person does that make them? Again, look at your own life, who have you hurt to get paid?

More importantly, think about the things you have done to make money that may have hurt someone else's life. Did you take them into consideration as you were doing what you were doing? Did you care about them or did you only think about you? Most probably you were only thinking about yourself. If you were not thinking about them—if you were making excuses to yourself for doing what you did, how does that fit into your religion? How does god view those actions?

Again, bringing this back to you, think about a time where you did something that hurt someone that had nothing to do with money. Truly think this through… Why did you do it? Most probably it was base in ego or power-tripping or you wanting something that they had. You did it. You hurt them. Where was your god and your religion in that action?

Here's the thing… Many people boldly claim they have no religion. Many people say, there is no god. Many people assert, they just don't care. They say that until they come up against the wall of their death. Then they do all they can to quash their guilt.

As I have long said, I find the Catholic Church one of the most interesting and appealing religious entities due to their process of forgiveness. In brief, you confess, you are given your penance, you do however many Hail Marys or Our Fathers on your rosary, and you are told you are freed from your sin. Though, according to Catholic doctrine, that may right you with god, that does not remove the pain you have caused to that someone else. They are still left hurting by what you did. Where is your religion, where is your god in all of that?

Nobody is perfect. We all make mistakes and we all do things that possibly hurts other people; whether intentional or not. But, if we do not monitor ourselves, if we do not catch ourselves, if we do not choose to stop ourselves, if we do not decide to try our hardest not to hurt anyone for any self-motivated reason, then how can we (how can you) ever be right with god?

You can cry out for forgiveness as you lay on your deathbed but should god provide you with forgiveness if you have hurt anyone and not tried to remedy your wrongs when you were active and healthy? Think about it, because we are all going to die someday. What will you be asking god for when you are breathing your last breaths?

* * *
21/Feb/2022 12:21 PM

Just because someone makes you laugh does not, necessarily, make them a good person.

One of My Photographs
21/Feb/2022 08:07 AM

For those of you out there who Yelp, you will understand that Yelp is a great method of emotional release. Sure, sure, you get to tell the world what you think about this restaurant or that business, but more than that, in the moment, you can express your feelings about a specific situation that is taking place. I see it as true psychotherapy. Yeah, some Yelpers are really negative people and only go on the attack. But, as we all know, people who exist on that plane of existence are lost to their own self-imposed damnation.

A kind of funny/telling note here is that: I've been Yelping for many years. And, I've been Yelp Elite for like eight years or something like that. It all started when some business did a shit job and did some really unprofessional stuff while cleaning one of my Rolex watches. But, anyway… On your Yelp profile, there is this section where you can tell the world a little bit about yourself and why people should read your reviews. They even have a place for your website; if you have one. I used to list mine there. The thing was, sometimes I would have a bad experience at a business or a restaurant and I would give them a one or two star review. Sometimes, after doing that, all of a sudden, I would have a bunch of bad reviews written about my books or my movies online. They would see my review, check out who wrote it, see I had a website, follow the links to my books and movies and stuff and then they would go on the attack. BAM! Review Revenge. …Not caring that maybe they created a bad experience in my life. But, isn't that how most people are? They don't care about what they do to you, they only care about what you do to them.

In another case, and this is one of the big problems with Yelp, there was this guy (or woman) who actually titled him or her self, Yelp Stalker, and they wrote a bunch of bad reviews about my creative stuff, without even viewing or reading them, on Amazon. That stuff is still up there on Amazon. You can check them out if you want. But yeah, that person titling themselves, Yelp Stalker, is an ideal example of how even I got stalked via my Yelp check-ins. I stopped doing that. It's dangerous. Too unsafe. I had a few weird experiences from people stalking where I would be via Yelp. (Oh shit, did I just make this person famous and give credibility to their negative doings?) Anyway...

But, more than writing a review about your feelings and your experiences at the various businesses, Yelp is a great place to show your photographic skills about the food you eat, the drink you drink, and what you see at the places you go to. I believe it really helps people make decisions. I know other people's reviews and photographs helps me make mine. Sometimes a business will even feature one of your photographs as a representation of their business, as they have with mine many times. The funny thing is... At least I see it as funny, sometimes they use photos that were taken years ago.

Just this morning, I get an alert from Yelp that one of my favorite Starbucks in Tokyo, in the Shinjuku district, スターバックスコーヒー 新宿三井ビル店, is using one of my photos as their main photo. I looked at the photograph and it made me smile. I totally remember taking it. But, I took it like five years ago. I don't know, is a photo taken that long ago and good representation of a business's life in this moment? I guess the big boss man (or woman) at that Starbucks believes that it is.

This is all a lot like life... We each have our experiences... We each live our experiences... We take mental notes of them and sometimes we even take photographs of them. This is the proof of where we were when. The proof to us and the proof to someone else. Mostly, all of this stuff is just kept within our own minds. But sometimes, someone grabs a piece of it/of us and likes it so much that they use it to describe something about and/or in them. This happens all the time when someone quotes someone else's song lyrics, poetry, or philosophy. But, here, but now, at least with me and that Starbucks in Shinjuku, somehow a photo taken all those years ago is decided to be an ideal representation of their HERE and their NOW??? Thanks! But, is it?

Think about it when you call up your memories. Is today yesterday?

The Things That I Do
20/Feb/2022 07:24 AM

    Here's an interesting little exercise for you that may provide you with some information about who and what you truly are and the direction your life is traveling towards.

    Make a list of the things that you don't do. We each have things that we refuse to do, and those things are in the forefront of our mind. These are not things that you do not like, for example, *"I don't like eggplant."* These are things that you consciously refuse to do. Take a moment and list them out. There is no right or wrong answer for this, this is simply a list of stuff you do not do.

    For example: I do not smoke. I do not drink alcohol. I don't drink coffee. I don't eat red meat. I am not judgmental of other people. I will not ride the bus. And, so on.

    Once this list is completed, make a list of the things that you do. Things that you do every day or a least quite frequently.

    For example: I exercise everyday. I smoke everyday. I drink coffee everyday. I drink a soft drink everyday. I am on the computer everyday. I look at social media on my phone everyday. I pray everyday. I kiss my children everyday.

    Again, there is no right or wrong answer for what you do or do not do. What you do and what you refuse to do are simply a depiction of who you have allowed yourself to become. And, you can take these lists as deeply as you want to take them or leave them as superficial as you wish.

    Each person in their life has the ability to guide themselves towards the ideal image of themselves. The problem is, most people spend very little energy in a quest towards self-realization. They simply are mindlessly guided towards become who they become by their family, their friends, and their society. Because of this, most people never become the best version of themselves that they could become. This is why this exercise is helpful. This is why this exercise allows you to take a look into what you have become and/or a view into who you do not want to be.

Make these lists. Take some time to really think them through. Once these lists are completed, with a clear mind, not defined by your own Mind Junk, ask yourself, *"Is this who I want to be?"* If it is, GREAT! If not, why not make the decision to change?

*   *   *
20/Feb/2022 07:05 AM

Sometimes one blanket is not enough.

Nirvana in a Mutt Shell
18/Feb/2022 02:31 PM

    Kinda funny… Today someone pointed me over in the direction of this new series of readings from the book I wrote, *Nirvana in a Nutshell*. They're up on YouTube. These readings and discourse are in Vietnamese. I'll pop a link to the first page of it for you down at the bottom of this blog. And, I already put one up over on my News page.
    I also found that there's a new page devoted to the Vietnamese translation of the book on-line. I'll put the link to that down at the bottom, as well.
    For some reason, *Nirvana in a Nutshell,* though it was never formally distributed in Vietnam, has done very well over there. For a number of years now, there have been translations of it circulating around that country and via the web in Vietnamese and it looks like there are a couple of in-print versions of it, as well. That's great! I'm glad the people of Vietnam find it inspiring. Sure, it may have been even greater if I had made some money from its Vietnamese distribution, as I am not a rich man. But, one way or the other, I'm glad the message in that book is appreciated, getting out there, and hopefully helping some people.
    My lady came home and walked over to me working here on the computer a little bit ago. I was in the process of showing her one of the pages on YouTube and when I was describing it I had one of those slips of the tongue and I said, *"Nirvana in a Mutt Shell."* We both laughed. I told her I would have to use that as a title for a blog. And, here it is…
    "Mutt Shell…" In so many ways, that's how I relate to spirituality. I am so about stepping away from the formality of religion, spiritualism, metaphysics, and/or whatever else and how ever else you may wish to refer to it. And, I speak about that a bit in *Nirvana in a Nut (Mutt) Shell.* …That you really have step beyond expected and previously

defined reality to find the truth of existence and the actuality of the Human Self.

I wrote *Nirvana in a Nutshell* a little over twenty years ago. I composed it when I had a lot of support from the editor at the then, highly influential publisher, Samuel Weiser, Inc., that later became Red Wheel/Weiser. Betty Lundsten was her name. She loved what I did and the minute one of my books was published she would ask me for another. I wish I had someone like that in my corner once again. Sadly, she passed away shortly after *Nirvana in a Nutshell* was published.

Overall, this book did and does really well. It was picked up by several other publishers and published in several languages across the globe. Nirvana in a Nutshell was really my attempt to help people understand that they (that you) can actually find and experience Nirvana.

At least for the people in Vietnam, I guess they really get it.

When things like this occur, it really makes me realize how people do not know who and what I truly am. A lot of people see me as just some guy who makes weird movies. Others see me as a martial artist or something like that. Sure, those are all things I do, but what I'm really about is enlightenment. ...About helping people find their center and transporting themselves to that more profound level of consciousness. That's what Nirvana in a <u>Mutt</u> Shell is all about.

Anyway... Sometimes life is interesting. And, I always thank the people who throw positive energy my direction. Thank you!!! I really do appreciate it!

If you feel like it, and if you have the inclination, check out *Nirvana in a Nutshell,* you may find something interesting in there.

* * *
18/Feb/2022 11:01 AM

Don't stand too close to someone who wants to punch you in the face.

* * *

18/Feb/2022 11:00 AM

Just because you dye your grey hair brown does not make you any younger.

The People Who Helped You
18/Feb/2022 08:21 AM

Think about a person who helped you sometime during your life. Think about a person who went out of their way to give you a hand to do something, to fix something, to become something that you wanted to become. How did you treat that person after the fact?

I really mean this... Take a moment and bring to mind someone who helped you do something or become something that you are today.

For me, a couple of people and/or incidents come to mind. I think to this time I got a flat tire. I was in a parking lot with my orange Porsche 914 up on the jack and I could not break the bolt loose. If you drive a car, and if you've tried to change a tire, you may know that sometimes the lug bolts when they are put on in the shop are done so with an air gun and the bolts are put on so tight that they are really hard to break loose. I've learned the trick to loosen the bolts when they are on very tight like that but this was a situation that took place a long time ago. Anyway, I was standing there with my girlfriend, I couldn't get the bolt loose, and I wasn't sure what to do. Up pulls this big burly guy. Seeing my plight, he gets out of his car and BAM he pops the bolts loose. Very nice gesture. I was so thankful for his help. Then, he just drove off.

I think to another time... I had been living next to this very bad, very loud neighbor; he just destroyed my life with all of his talking and all of his crazy noise. Post a confrontation I had with him, the manager of the building I lived in, knowing this other guy was the one at fault, suggested I move into this different apartment. A place with a specular view. She were giving me a gift. *"Thank you!"* I accepted the offer. The only problem was, it was mid-week and I could find no one to help me move my stuff. I would have paid someone, but I didn't know who to pay as how do

I explain I was just moving from one apartment to another. The move was really trying and traumatic. Again, that neighbor by creating a situation where I had to move really fucked my life up. But, I got it done. The problem was, after doing it, I was just spent. ...My new next-door neighbor, a nice guy and his wife and his daughter from India, he knocks on my door with a pecan pie. I didn't even know how to express my thanks. Though I don't have much of a sweet tooth, the gesture was so nice. That was the best pie I ever ate.

These may be considered small things. But, sometimes small things truly set a person's life in a new and better direction.

Then, there were people like Don Jackson who also stepped up to help my life. Though we had a complicated and sometimes confrontational relationship, he cared enough about me, as a person, to actually do something for me. In situations like that, it is what you do with the help you are given that creates the next element of your life. What I did, from that relationship, was to move forward and become the filmmaker I have become. For better or for worse, he helped me in my becoming. Though he certainly had his enemies, I, like you, must define what a person like that gave me and be appreciative for what I was later allowed to achieve due to my interaction with them. This is how you must define relationships like that, as well.

So many times, I witness people who are helped by someone and later they go after that person and truly mess with their life. They do this via words and other actions. But, is that the right thing to do? In many cases, these people would not even have a platform if it were not for the person they are attacking. They would not even be able to do what they are doing if that person had not helped in guiding them and showing them the way.

When I see a person attacking someone who has helped them, regardless of their motivation, I always understand that they possess a flaw in their character. Because, if they did not have that person's help initially, they would not be where they are today. Yet, there they are attacking that person who helped them; attempting to hurt their life. How can that be right?

I always discuss how people are a selfish entity. At least many of them are. But, it doesn't have to be that way. Instead, you can be that big burly guy who take the time to stop, hop out of his car, and breaks my tire bolts loose. You can be the person who buys someone a pie simply to welcome them to the neighborhood. But, if you attack those who have helped create you—if you defame those people who helped to make you what you have become, what does that say about you? Sure, you may no longer like the person. For example, there were years when Don and I barely spoke. But, beyond all that, there was the person who wanted and actually tried to help me. You always must keep that in mind. That must be the final definition of how you remember them.

So again, think about someone who has helped you. Remember them for what they gave to your life. What did you give back to their life? Do you speak of them kindly? Do you tell people about what they did for you? Or, because you have become the something that you became, do you try to diminish them because of who you now are?

Think about it… Think about how some people speak negatively about other people—those people who helped them become who and what they are. Think about how you speak about other people—those who helped you. You can really learn a lot about who a person truly is and if you should even consider hanging out with them. Because how a person speaks about someone else will be how they will speak about you.

Praise those who have helped you, even if you don't like them anymore. Because without their help you would not be who you have become.

Trying to Fix the Song
18/Feb/2022 07:19 AM

  For those of you out there who are musicians, you will understand that sometimes you record a piece of music and though you really like it there is something just not perfect about it. For you traditional musicians, you may record it and record it again and again until you get it as close to right as you can. For the kind of music I create, Zen Jazz, you really can't go back and do it over and over and over again, however, because what was done was already done and that it that. If I redid it, all I would get is something different. This being said, there are times when I like the essence of the piece I recorded but something is just not quite right about it so I will try to fix it in the remix. Sometimes this can take a very long time and sometimes is doesn't work at all and I have to let it go. That's what happened to a recent piece of music I was working on. A lot of time and hope, but it just did not come together. That's kind of like life, I guess? You try and you try but sometimes there is nothing you can do to get the results you desire.
  Recently, I have been rediscovering some of the music I have, created by other people, on reel-to-reel tape. Most of you are probably too young to remember this but back in the late '60s and early '70s, for those who really wanted to listen to music in its purest form, that would be via tapes played on reel-to-reel decks. Check out some of the movies of that era and you will see what I'm talking about. Music on reel-to-reel really possesses a unique quality. Not only would the music have been recorded on tape but it was directly transferred to tape. From this, and because of this, it just possesses this unique element of sound. If you have the money and the time and the desire, I suggest you go out and find a high quality, working, reel-to-reel deck and buy some tapes of some of the great music created in that era and give

a listen. I think you will understand what I am speaking about.

Around that time, music on tape began to transition. The 8-Track player was released. I always joke, I'm the last person on earth who owns a working 8-Track player. But, I know there are other people out there, as well, who enjoy listening to music played on one of those decks. In fact, one of my neighbors has an insane 8-Track collection that he is really proud of. I was always kind of surprised when the resurgence of music cassette tapes occurred, a number of years ago, that 8-Tracks didn't reemerge, as well. I mean, 8-Tracks are so much cooler. But, I guess they fell from grace before the cassettes so there were and are a lot more cassette decks available. For those of us who are old enough, we can remember transferring LPs to cassette tape to listen to that music in our cars and stuff and, of course, *"Mix tapes,"* are always referenced in movies. But again, if you have the inclination, you should find a working 8-Track deck and pick up some tapes. There was actually a much larger variety and a lot more music disseminated on 8-Track tape than on reel-to-reel. I even have this still unwrapped, unopened Neil Young 8-Track tape, that I've been hiding away for years, until the moment is right to open it and play it. Again, the quality of the sound of 8-Track sound is very definitive for those with an ear for such things.

Speaking of Neil Young, last night I was rewatching a little bit of that movie Johnathan Deeme did about a concert given by Neil Young at the Ryman Auditorium titled, *Heart of Gold*. At one point, Neil Young talks about the guitar he owns and was playing and how it originally belonged to Hank Williams. Wow, how great would that be to be able to play a guitar once owned by Hank Williams? I guess you'd have to have a lot of money to own something like. But, what great vibes that guitar must hold. What a great feeling that guitar must possess. ...Or, even to be able to play a guitar owned by Neil Young. But, anyway...

I think most of our lives are defined by music. From the time we are born, music is everywhere. Every store you go into is playing it, every car radio on the street, and the list goes on and on. Some of us create music. It can be such a freeing and uplifting spiritual meditation to create music—even if you don't record it. I know throughout my teens and deep into my twenties, I would sit for hours-upon-hours playing the guitar. Many times, to no one else's ears but by my own.

Recording changes everything. But, that's what ushers music towards eternity. How music is recorded really defines its sound. The method in which it is listened to really defines it, as well. Sure, it's really easy now to pull up music on your phone or your smart device. And yeah, you will get to hear that song you like instantaneously. But, there is really a deeper element to music. There is a mysticism within the sound if you take the time to listen for it. How you get it delivered to your ears also creates, alters, and defines the entire experience. Take a moment, listen to the subtle structure of the sound when you hear the music. There is magic hidden within its realms. Try it; take the time to listen to it via a new, all be it old, format, you may be amazed at what you discover.

The "I'm Not Sorry" Factor
17/Feb/2022 07:28 AM

Have you ever had some random thing happen to you, something happened out of nowhere, and you were really sorry it happened? Maybe you slipped or fell and broke a bone. It really hurt. You never saw it coming. You are so sorry that it happened as it is going to take you some time to heal. But, you knew what happened, you were there to witness it, maybe you even understood why it happened, so you could rationalize it. You are sorry for all things concerned with the situation but that is natural, it is you and you are the one feeling what you are feeling.

Have you ever witnessed something hurtful happen to someone you care about? Maybe they fell and hurt themselves. Maybe something came out of nowhere and injured them. You didn't do it. You didn't cause it to happen. But, because you care about them you are so sorry it happened to them. Maybe you even feel responsible because you were in their company when it occurred. You are sorry about the situation but that is natural because you really care about them.

Then, there are the, *"Not Sorry,"* people. The people who do something to someone else and just don't care. Have you ever encountered a situation like that? Have you ever had someone hurt you or hurt your life and they just don't give a fuck? What motivates a person like that? We can assume that they are a selfish and self-centered individual but that does not excuse their behavior.

I know there have been people who have hurt my life and tried to turn the blame of the situation around on me. Perhaps that has happened to you, as well? It doesn't feel good. In fact, it probably hurts more because you witness a person who has hurt you or your life and then they are so selfish that they refuse to own their responsibility in the situation.

I've spoken about the people who have hurt me in this blog over the years. ...People who were totally at fault but then either lied or denied and try to blame me for what they did. Has that happened to you?

The sad truth of life is, sometimes bad things happen to good people. But, who did those bad things? It was a person, motivated by their whatever, who unleashed that pain. They may have gained from that action of the hurting of someone else, but what does that make them? Nothing more than an individual who hurts the life of others. Then, when something bad happens to them, they question, *"Why me?"* But, the answer to that question is obvious. If you've hurt someone and you have not corrected or at least tried to correct that pain then that hurt goes on forever and ever. The person you hurt will always hold ill will towards you. Why would they (would you) think that a repercussion is not in the cosmic works?

Let's take a moment and bring one or more of these hurtful situations clearly into mind. Think about a time when you got physically hurt. Maybe you fell, maybe you cut yourself, maybe something like a bicycle, motorcycle, or car accident happened to you and you were injured. Relive that moment. Relive the moments just before that situation occurred. What happened? Why did it happen? Who's fault was it? Was the fault yours, someone else's, or maybe a combination of more than one person? Really chart this out. Who did you blame? Did you blame yourself? Or, did you blame someone else? Truly get to the bottom of this. Was it your fault or was it their fault? Why did you blame who you blamed? Did you blame them to remove yourself of any responsibility? And, if you did, why did you do that? Moreover, what did that casting of blame do to the life of that other person? Really think this through as what you may learn will be very revelatory. You can replace an emotional injury for a physical injury in this exercise if you want.

Now, let's turn this around. Truly investigate a situation where you did something that hurt the life of another person. Whether your actions were intentional or not is almost unimportant. You did what you did and they were hurt. How did you feel about that? Did you care? Did you feel sorrow for the pain you caused? Did you try to fix the damage you created? Or, did you lie to yourself and to others about what you instigated? Did you look for the support of friends to tell you what you did was okay? Did you make excuses for what you caused? Really! Chart this situation out in your mind. Don't be afraid of the fact that you may, (possibly), come to a harsh conclusion.

We all know the experience of hurt and pain. We all know the feeling when someone we care about is hurt or injured in the many ways that can come at a person. But, how much time do you spend thinking about the pain you caused to someone else compared to how much time you focus on your own pain? How much time do you spend trying to fix any pain you caused someone else? But, most importantly, if you take pride in the hurting of someone else, if you hurt someone else intentionally, you are a bad person and bad things will come your direction. Don't lie to yourself about the fact that this will occur.

We all get hurt in life. We all remember the pain we have felt. We all know when people we care about get hurt. We feel for their pain. But, what about all the people that cause this pain, who are they, why are they, and why are they allowed to continue hurting other people?

If you are a person who has hurt someone, especially if you have done so intentionally, you should be ashamed of yourself. If you're not, you should be ashamed of that.

The world only gets better when we each own our deeds. The world only gets better when we, personally, never hurt anyone intentionally and when and if we do hurt someone unintentionally, we do all we can to undo any pain we have caused.

What have you done? Who have you hurt? What are you going to do about it?

Chasing Backwards
16/Feb/2022 07:30 AM

  I don't know if you know this about me, but I pretty much do all of my own everything. For better or for worse, that's who I am. I remember I once knew this guy who was really high up in the financial game and one day I asked him, *"Can't you just have your secretary do that?"* His answer was, *"Why do I need a secretary? Then you have to explain everything to someone else and they usually do it wrong."* I don't know if I'm that dogmatic, I would love to have a helper, but as it has turned out I'm always the one who seems to be the person who has to do all of my own everything. If I want it done, I'm the one who has to learn how to do it and get 'er done. I film and I edit my own movies. I take photographs and design my posters, movie, music, and book covers. I design my own websites. Of course, I do my own music for soundtracks and all of the other etc… If I want it done, it seems I'm the only one who cares enough to get it done. Sure, I guess I could pay someone but like my friend said, *"They usually do it wrong…"* Anyway…

  As we all know, with time, technology changes. Sometimes with that change the changes that change we don't really like. For example, I know I used to love the original iMovie. You could really do some great stuff with the early release(s) of that program. Then came OS 10 and it was gone. Sure, with the new school version of the program you have some new options, but some really important somethings were lost. And, what was lost cannot be replaced. I miss the way it was in that back then.

  Recently, with the new chips they put in the new Macs, one of the essential plugins I use in the design of websites no longer functions. That plugin was a really essential component to certain pages on my website. But, with the new Macs, I can no longer use it. And, as the designer of that plugin has checked out from the stratosphere and the new owners are not going to upgrade the plugin to work on the new Macs my only option would be to go backwards and buy an older refurbished Mac if I hoped to continue to do what I want to continue to do.

I spoke to my lady about this, and she said, *"You are chasing backwards." "Chasing Backwards,"* interesting phrase. I told her, *"I'm going to have to steal that."* And, here it is…

You know, as you get older you really possess the time to witness the change in places and in the things of reality. What you once loved may no longer be there. I know there are so many restaurants I used to love to go to, now they are gone. And, that's just one example. So many of the stores I loved are gone, as well. Especially some GREAT bookshops. Technology, forget about it… As it changes so fast, in the blink of an eye it is gone. But, every time something good is gone, then what? Is what you are left with actually better? Sure, it is different. Sure, for the new generation, it may be all they know. But, when something is gone then it is gone. When that something was loved and used and desired and it is taken from us, then what? What are we supposed to do? Because it was certainly not our choice that they took it away.

Sometimes, for a moment, we are sometimes allowed to chase backwards; get another one of that something we once had. But then, eventually, those are gone as well. You can only chase backwards so long because sooner or later you too will be gone.

Chase backwards or continually change and move forward… That's the question. What's the answer?

* * *

15/Feb/2022 04:49 PM

If you sit back and watch your time pass, it will pass and then it will be gone.

If you sit back and don't notice your time passing, your time will pass just the same.

Your time is here and then it is gone.

What are you doing with your time to make your time worthwhile?

The Position of Peace
14/Feb/2022 10:56 AM

Most people never truly understand the experience of peace. Yes, from time-to-time they may feel happiness due to the fact that life is going in the direction that they want, and their needs and desires are being fulfilled. But, that is not true peace. That is, at best, momentary contentment. The true experience of peace is much different from that. It is an expansive awareness of inner serenity.

Why do most people never experience true peace? The reason is most likely that, due to the fact they have never felt it, they have never developed a pathway to embrace its practice. Let's change that.

First of all, you must identify the feeling of true peace if you hope to reexperience it. Let's look for that feeling within your list of possible experiences.

Think about a time when you had perhaps dosed off to sleep for just a moment. Then, you woke up, and in that moment, somewhere just between the realms of sleep and awake awareness, there was that second of profound contentment. That's the feeling. Maybe you were somewhere in a place such as the mountains or on the beach or you were looking out over the horizon and all of a sudden, your thoughts just fell away, and the sense of profound awareness and peace overcame you. That's the feeling. Maybe you were petting your cat and they were purring or holding your dog and the two of you just fell into pure contentment and based upon your interaction all of the pains of the world feel away. That's the feeling.

Once you feel true peace, you know it exists. But, due to the ways and the distractions of the world, it is very hard to reclaim it. Certainly, meditation is pathway to experience inner peace. But, meditation, by its very design, is a corridor to mindful mindlessness. Thus, meditation is not an absolute passageway to experience a sensation.

Let's take a look at where the feeling of true peace emanates from on your body. If you have felt it, particularly if you were laying down, you will know that there is an energy that emanate from the region of your solar plexus when you encounter this feeling. In Sanskrit, this location is known as the Manipura Chakra. Via traditional teachings and the oftentimes misunderstood explanations of the chakras, this location is often defined as the location of personal power or the lack thereof. But, that is far too simple of an description. This location is also at the center of the body which is the location from which all internal power emanates. In addition to the fact, this bodily location is just a small distance from the Heart Chakra, *"Anahata"* in Sanskirt, making it a central point of human function and emotional existence. Moreover, the defined locations of the chakras have come to be far too stagnate. As each person is a unique example of human evolution, each person is a creature onto themselves and, as such, each person possesses their own unique example of the human experience. Thus, for each of us, the location of the elimination of the feeling of true inner peace is somewhat different. But, most commonly, it originates from this region of the body. This is just something to keep in mind. Not a fact but simply a thought.

True peace is a physical, mental, and emotional embracing of a state of mind that allows the individual to reconnect with the better, purer, and more true and refined self. Why shouldn't we all be allowed to experience true peace all the time? Answer: The world and the way in which we were taught to encounter and live life. But, it does not have to be that way.

So, let's try an exercise. If you can, lay down. If you can't right now, just keep this exercise in mind and try it when you can.

Lay down, close your eyes. Let all things be as all things are. Just let go.

Note: You are not trying to meditate here so don't attempt to force your thoughts out of your brain. Just let them flow in a calm and passive manner. Do not force anything. In your letting go, let go. If you want to focus on the Manipura Chakra region of your body, you can. But, you don't have to. Don't necessary seek and look for a time when you felt peace, like say when you were looking at the horizon, just let it all go. Let everything go. Be where you are how you are.

One of the things that I always find when I do this exercise is that may hands are often pulsating with energy. I guess that's due to the fact that I am one of those people who is very, *"On,"* and always doing something, and that is where much of the energy of my body focuses itself. But, each person is different. Your energy may focus on and emanate from another part of your body. Wherever it is, feel that energy and let it naturally dissipate. As you do this, just let your mind be free. Let it feel like you are falling asleep. If you do fall asleep, that's fine. Don't fight anything.

As you enter this space of peaceful consciousness, let it happen. Find that place in you where that peace dwells. There is no absolute definition for its location. As stated, we are each unique example of human life. Just let it come to you. Just let it be. Feel the consciousness of peace.

Most people never try to consciously encounter this experience and that is why they don't feel it. You can be different, however. You can take the time to develop a friendship with peace. If you do, you will know its feeling very well and you will, via each new encountering, develop a deeper and deeper understand of what true peace feels like and, thought time and practice, you will be able to call it up a will.

Be peaceful. Try it. Your entire life may become better.

The Zen Speed Flick
13/Feb/2022 03:50 PM

    For whatever it's worth, I am a member of the Academy and an active member of SAG/Aftra. As such, and as we are in awards season, I am given screener copies of a lot of movies every year to view in order to vote for them to win the various awards they are nominated for. I was a member of the SAG Awards nominating committee for a time, as well, but that's a whole other story...

    I get all these movies every year, big packets, but I watch very few. I've either already seen the movies I wanted to see or, the few that I haven't yet seen but I have a desire to view, I sit back, stick it in the DVD player, and try to watch.

    I don't know about you, but I find it very-very hard to watch a movie that I don't want to watch. I remember hearing famed movie reviewers talking on talk shows describing how they get up and watch movies all day long every day and sometimes deep into the night. *"It's my job,"* they would say. A lot of those movies they really disliked. I just can't do that! I watch a few minutes of a film and if it is not touching the certain spot in me, I just turn it off. Life is too short to watch something I don't want to watch.

    Just a funny note (or two)... I had cast this actress in one of my films a number of years ago and she was very good. She invited me to see the screening of another film she had acted in. Sure! I grabbed one of my filmmaking friends and we went. The film was showing at a screening room over at Raleigh Studios in Hollywood. The only problem was, the film sucked beyond belief. My friend was willing to sit through it (I think), just not to cause a scene. Me, I said, we really need to leave. I let him pick the moment. He taps me when. BAM, we get up and we are gone. Never heard from that actress again. Sad, I would have used her in other films.

Another time, I was invited to a screening of a Troma film. Lloyd Kaufman, the man behind Troma and the director of the film, was there. The film was screening at a big theater over on the U.S.C. campus. The movie was about to begin. My lady and I sat down in the back row. Lloyd came and sat down one row up, directly in front of us. The movie begins. Damn it was bad! Pure Troma. A few minutes in, I just couldn't take in. I hated to do it with Lloyd right there, but I had to get up and leave. I snuck out as quietly as possible, but I saw Lloyd taking notice. Oh well, I guess no Troma films for me. ☺

Anyway… Last night, I stuck *House of Gucci* in the old DVD player. I, of course, heard a lot of hype about the film. And, Ridley Scott, the director, has directed some great movies. I'm a big fan. This one, at least as far as I'm concerned, was not so great. Also, it seemed way too long. …Doesn't it seem like the time clock on more and more movies has grown and grown—they seem to just be way longer than way back in the way back when. Too long…

Which leads me to the point of all this: *The Zen Speed Flick*.

What is a *Zen Speed Flick?* A movie cut down to its most essential elements.

To be fair, and to give credit where credit is due, I was not the one to first envision *The Zen Speed Flick*, that was Don Jackson. But, he really wasn't an editor. So, it was me who put the idea into practice. And, I think it is a good one. …Cut that movie down to maybe fifteen or twenty minutes. Just the best of the best. That way, the audience gets the entire experience of the film but cut down to a palatable package. I've done that with several of Don and my and my films: *Max Hell Frog Warrior, Samurai Vampire Bikers from Hell, Guns of El Chupacabra,* and *Super Hero Central* just to name a few. I mean, with this, you get to see the movie and remove all the boring bullshit. So many times, even with high budget extravaganzas like, *House of Gucci,* I wish they would just cut it down to size.

Anyway, that's just my thoughts… My thoughts on cinema for the day, if you will. I mean, a lot of things should be cut down to size, not just movies but TV shows, music, articles, conversations, and even blogs like this.

PS: Let me tell you a secret… Yeah, I'm supposed to vote, one way or the other, for those films they send me… …Don't tell anyone, but I never do.

* * *
13/Feb/2022 07:38 AM

Are you listening for the noise or are you listening for the silence?

* * *
13/Feb/2022 07:37 AM

The more water you put in a pot the longer it takes to boil.

*   *   *
                                11/Feb/2022 02:02 PM
If you wait long enough, everything will be gone.

Face-to-Face
11/Feb/2022 07:31 AM

Ever since the world has been infected with this COVID-19 Coronavirus Pandemic, people have become separated. You couldn't go here; you couldn't go there. People began to communicate more and more from afar. It kept people safe, I guess? …With less interaction, there is less chance to get infected.

People began to work from home. My lady has been working from home for two years now; ever since the first shut down. We set her up an office and now, like so many others, she does conferences via Zoom and other apps like that and takes meetings on the phone all day long, while her face is staring into the computer screen, *"Playing with board games,"* as I jokingly define what she is doing.

It's changing, little by little, I guess. …Going somewhere in the direction of the way it used to be. But, it ain't over yet. And, who knows when it will be?

Sometimes people ask me if I'm teaching classes via Skype or Zoom? Answer: No, I haven't taught any classes or given any seminars since this whole thing began. I've been asked by a few schools if I wanted to. But, it's just not me.

Ever since the dawning of the internet; when first there was posting boards, then chat rooms, on to video calls and video conferencing, I've never done any of that. I've never even had Skype or Zoom. I haven't used it once. I've only done Facetime once I think. I don't even like to email or message as words and ideas, via those passageways, are so often misconstrued. Even when my doctor asks if I want to do a tele-chat for my appointments, I tell her that I rather do an in-person. I mean, why should I pay all that money for health insurance if I can't communicate in person?

I remember back to a time many-many years ago. I was a teenager. I had been phone introduced to the female cousins of one of my friends. The girl and I immediately hit it off. As we were young, and she lived a long way from Hollywood, in the greater L.A. area, we had no way of personally meeting. But, I would speak with her for hours-upon-hours. You know how it is, all those feelings of infatuation that you can possess when you are a teenager. This went on for a time, when I finally met her sometime (a long time) later, I felt absolutely no chemistry with her at all. Though I once believed I loved her, face-to-face, there was nothing. What does this tell us about life and a life not lived face-to-face?

    I know separation from family and friends and people, in general, has been one of the biggest complaints throughout this pandemic. It has created a lot of problems. Problems that would not have existed if the world had it not been globally attacked. Thanks China! And, thanks to all you unvaccinated people for keeping this pandemic alive and thriving! But, like in all things life, you are defined by the reality that surrounds you. Yes, you can try to fight your way out. Yes, you can try to change it, as it affects you. But, the fact of the fact is, this pandemic has illustrated to all of us the truth of living; which is, at the root of life, none of us possess very much control.

    Some people adapt very well to living a life alone. Some people are fine with viewing life through and via their computer screen or their iPhone all day long. Me, I guess I'm just too Old School. I like life lived, face-to-face. That's just me. I don't want to teach a class where there is no personal interaction. I just don't like hanging out with people when I don't know what is going on below camera view. Really? Who is on the other side of the computer screen and what is actually going on? Person-to-person, that's life. That's living. That's interacting. That's me. How about you?

When You Know More Than Your Teacher
09/Feb/2022 12:30 PM

Have you ever been in one of those situations where you realize, *"Wow, I know way more about this subject than this person who is teaching me?"* Sometimes this comes from a position of arrogance. Sometimes it arises from a position of ego. Other times, however, the fact of the fact is, maybe you do know more than the person who is teaching you.

If you ever find yourself in this position, it can get pretty complicated. I mean, what do you do? If you stand up and tell them they are wrong, confrontation can arise. So, is being silent the best option?

Being involved with the martial arts for virtually my entire life, I have witness, first-hand, how respect and the lack thereof can come into play. As a student, I always studied under the direction of Asian born instructors. There was always a feeling that them, being from Asia, held some mystical and profound knowledge. ...They had some secret, mysterious something that we Westerners could never genuinely comprehend.

I have watched as some of the teachers from Asia really played on this belief. They took advantage of this assumed understanding. In fact, some really took advantage of other people based on this certainty.

It took me a long time to conclude that they didn't possess any hidden knowledge expect for possibly the fact that they came of age in a different culture which made them perceive the world in a differing manner from those of us born in the West.

In the martial arts, the teaching of respect towards your instructors and other practitioners is paramount to the training. Yet, look around the Western world and all you will see is a lot of insults in the martial arts. A lot of people believing they know more than that whomever else who is teaching that whatever else. The fact is, this goes entirely against the teachings of the martial arts. And, if a person behaves in this manner, it illustrates that they are not a true martial artist. Yet, aside from all the insults thrown, there have been seminar instructors attacked from behind while they were imparting their knowledge. There have been apprentices who have stolen the pupils of their instructors. There have even been challenges to combat. But, why? Answer: It is all based on one person believing that they possess more knowledge than a teacher.

    I remember a number of years ago I was close with this young lady who was attending college. She was taking a course on anthropology and the instructor was praising the teachings of Carlos Castaneda. Probably most of you out there don't even know who Carlos Castaneda was. In a different time, he was a highly read, revered, and believed person who supposedly studied Mexican mysticism under a Yaqui shaman named, Don Juan. This thing is, all of what he wrote was proven to be fabricated. Even his dissertation he composed to impart earn his doctorate from U.C.L.A. was proven to be based on nothing more than concoctions created within his own mind. I gave the girl a couple of books that were written by Castaneda's critics. The next time she was in class and the teacher was speaking his tributes to the man, she contradicted him, really taking him down with the knowledge she had obtain from myself and to a greater degree those books. The result? A bad grade in the course. Lesson Learned? It may not be a good thing to attack your teachers.

    The thing is, that teacher knew what he thought he knew. The girl, she knew what she thought she knew. He had his references, she had hers. So, who was ultimately right? And, if someone believes something to be true, even if you tell them they are wrong, who is truly the, *"Knower."*

    Whenever you study anything from anybody, it is important to know beforehand the source of their knowledge. Who they are, where they went to school, who they got their training from, and, more importantly, why they are teaching what they are teaching in the first place.

There is a lot of ego attached to a person who is teaching anything. You really need to take that into consideration before you ever sit before them and take their class. This is especially the case if you are learning from someone who is teaching outside of an established system of knowledge.

Knowing is knowing. But, what knowing truly is, simply involves believing. You can believe what you are learning is true, but that does not necessarily make it true. You can think your instructor is great. Or, you can believe you know more than they do. No matter how you shuffle the cards, at the end of the day, all that matters is what have you learned. Are you humble enough to learn, even from someone you believe knows less than you? If not, why do you need to study anything at all?

* * *
09/Feb/2022 12:30 PM

If you insult a person one time you should pay them ten compliments.

Do You Ever Tell Yourself That You are Sorry?
08/Feb/2022 07:42 AM

Whenever you hurt someone else in some way the expected action is to say, *"I'm sorry,"* and try to repair any damage that you instigated. At least it should be. This is how people with a conscience behave. Action equals reactions equals apology. But, when you do something that hurts yourself, do you ever apologize to yourself?

Most people do what they do in life. As stated, if they do something hurtful to someone else, they say that they are sorry and try to move forward and not do something like that again. However, when someone does something to themselves that hurts their body, mind, life, or lifestyle in someway they most commonly just sweep it under the carpet of life and try to forget it as quickly as possible. The problem with this style of mental behavior is, people do a lot of things that truly hurts their own life and their own life evolution but never consciously acknowledge it. They never trace its root cause to the source. And, they do nothing to remedy the problem they instigated. From this, a lot of what could or should have been in a person's life is never realized.

There was this movie made a few years back titled, *The Last Movie Star*. It's a piece starring an aging Burt Reynolds as a grumpy former movie star going to receive an award at a very small film festival. The movie is interesting in that it intercuts footage from Reynold's heyday where he interacts with his younger self in scenes from movies like, *Smokey and the Bandit*. A one point he says to his younger self, *"I wish I could give you some advice because you are about to make some bad life choices."* As we all know that is what he did.

In spiritual circles there is often the propagated belief that, *"Everything is perfect," "It all is as it should be,"* but this is just another way to make excuses for someone to not look at their own life with any depth of perception. Again, it's easy to see the hurt you cause in someone else. But, when it comes to yourself, it is far more common to not want to take a hard look.

Take a moment right now... Think about a time when you made an obvious mistake in your life. A situation when you said, *"Yes,"* when you should have said, *"No."* A time when you turned right when you should have turned left. Clearly bring that moment into focus. Think about and explore what that choice did to your life. Though obviously things can never truly be different from what they are, pretend for a moment and think about how your life could have and would have been different if you did not do what you did.

Now, that the moment is clearly in your mind, walk your way through to the other side of it. Know that it happened, understand that you made the choice that created it, and truly tell yourself that you are sorry. Truly express sorrow and remorse that you did what you did to yourself. Ask yourself for forgiveness.

Nothing in life, once it is done, can be undone. But, what can happen after the fact is learning to never do something wrong or hurtful again. This is taking the path of conscious life evolution.

If you do not address an issue, if you do not consciously understand what you did was wrong, and that what you did hurt your life, you may continue to make the same mistakes. Is that what you want to do?

We all make mistakes. We all do things that hurts others and that hurts ourselves. But, you can be better. You can do better. You can, if you are willing to.

Consciously forgive yourself. Knowingly, say you're sorry to yourself. Do it and mean it. Try to fix any damage you've created. Know never to do it again. And, move forward in your life a better and more aware example of a human being.

What You Do with Your Time to Make Your Money
07/Feb/2022 08:40 AM

I was watching the documentary, *The Tinder Swindler* on Netflix last night. It was about this guy who would meet woman on Tinder and then get them to finance his elaborate lifestyle by making promises of love, friendship, and all that kind of stuff that sucks a woman (at least a woman in the case of this documentary) in. This guy lived an elaborate lifestyle! He was jetting across the globe in private jets, living in 5-Star hotels, and just existing in excess, all on the money of these women he met on Tinder. One of the first things I thought while watching it was, that must take a lot of time to play all those women to get enough money to live that large.

You know, there is this illusion that living that large it somehow the great goal. And sure, traveling first class across the globe is, in some cases, way better than living in a dumpy place with no hope of betterment. That's why I was constantly traveling in the '80s. My life, *"Out there,"* on the, *"Hard Road,"* as I labeled it, was far better than my life at home.

The thing is, that's what this guy offered those woman, the chance to live the promise of that dream. Isn't that what every man or woman offers a potential partner; to live that dream of that of something better?

But, what does your life really equal if all you do is nothing more than trying to find that next dollar—however you try to find it? I mean, think how many people work day-in and day-out just trying to survive. Like the old saying goes, *"You work and then you die."* This guy's hustle was no less arduous. He had to be constantly on the make.

The thing is, it all comes down to how you make your money and who you get your money from. Being in the film industry for decades now, I have seen some really underhanded shit. Where do you think the money to make the small or the insane budget films come from? Rarely, any part of it comes from the filmmaker themselves. It comes from the promises made to people with money about making more money. But, rarely do the investors ever make a dime. Sure, some people have money to burn. But, where did that money come from? How did they get that money? Who had to, *"Work,"* to generate the space where that money would be produced? Who paid the price for that money?

In the doc they featured just a few women who this guy got his money from. But, this guy was living so large, for so long, that there had to be hundreds of others. They just didn't come forward. Yeah, the guy finally got caught but he only did a few months in jail. Then, as the documentary shows, he was/is back out and living very-very large. Again, where is he getting the money? He is not earning it in the traditional sense.

You have to ask yourself, what does a life like that actually equal? Yeah, you party your brains out and, sure, that's fun. But, is that the definition of a life well lived?

In the doc they showed how this guy came up from humble beginnings in Israel. So yes, he rose above the limitations of his youth. But, so did Gene Simmons.

Now, I was never really a fan of KISS, so all you KISS fans out there don't hate on me. I'm just using Gene Simmons as an example. He rose out of less than ideal circumstances after being born in Israel. But, he did something with his life. He created something. He has lived an elaborate lifestyle, but he gave something back. He gave the world music that millions of people love. And, he continues to do it. That is a karmic exchange.

The point of all this is that we all need to look at what we are doing with our life and our life time. We all need to look at how we are earning our living, leading to what we do with the money we earn, no matter from what source that money comes in. We need to be good and we need to be conscious in the way we make our livelihood, no matter how well we are allowed to live via the money we have earned.

What are you doing to get your money? How are you getting your money? Why is anyone giving you money? And, what is the karmic after-effect on the people who have provided you with that money to live the way you live? Who are you helping? Who are you hurting? If you don't think about this, you are a selfish person. If you do think about this and you don't care, you are nothing more than a swindler.

* * *
07/Feb/2022 07:32 AM

If you are invisible, no one can see you.

If you are invisible, then you are free.

*   *   *
07/Feb/2022 07:09 AM

Constructive criticism is still just criticism.

What is criticism?

It is you deciding that you know what is better for another person than what they know is best for themselves.

* * *
05/Feb/2022 05:17 PM

The news is temporary.

*   *   *
05/Feb/2022 02:40 PM

Some people think that being bad is cool and edgy. That is until something bad is done to them.

The Goodness in Your Heart
05/Feb/2022 08:09 AM

The question is, *"Is there goodness in your heart?"*

Why are you doing what you are doing? Do you ever question yourself before you do?

Do you care about the answer to that question? And, if you do, does it ever make you change your mind?

The problem with people is that they do what they do motivated by their own personal motivations. But, the problem of doing from this perspective is that in that doing the only doing is done for the self, even if that doing is an attempted doing for someone else. Meaning, doing from that perspective, no matter how much your mind may tell you it is your doing done for someone else, is very selfish. Is selfishness ever a good things?

Take a moment and truly ponder what was the last thing that you did. What was the last thing that you decided to do and saw it through to its competition? Whether this was some physical action or some words spoken, truly investigate what did you do?

My guess would be that when you did it you did not even think about why you were about to do it. A thought or an idea or an emotion just came to your mind and you followed through with that thought or idea. Living your life from this perspective, however, leaves all things in a constant state of flux where there is no absolute consciousness or precise structure to your doing. Things are just done. Maybe they come out good, maybe they come out bad, maybe you don't care about how they come out as you are already on the road to your next undefined doing.

Sure, we all want what we want in any specific moment. The current fantasy. But, how long does any of that last?

Maybe your doing gets the reaction <u>you</u> want but what does your doing do to anyone or anything else? Do you take the time to contemplate that before you do? Because all doing does something to somebody.

A true life, a good life, comes down to a life that is defined by positive doing. Meaning, all that you do equals positive results.

How much of what you have said or done has equaled positive results? How much of what you have said or done has equaled negative results? And, have you/do you ever contemplate any of this before you do or after what you have done is done? If you don't, the definition of your life is clear. If you only think about yourself and what <u>you</u> are feeling, and you allow this to motivate your words and actions, the definition of your life is clear.

So, what are you going to do about any of this? Is there goodness in your heart? Truly, is there? If you believe there is, then how will this guide you to chart your next actions. Are you simply going to continue to do, motivated by whatever is momentarily in your mind? Or, are you going to take the time to chart out your actions and unleash only the positive which hurts no one and no thing and makes all things better? Is there goodness in your heart?

* * *

05/Feb/2022 07:27 AM

Never tempt anyone with money because if you do they will almost universally choose that over you.

The Internet is a Strange Thing
04/Feb/2022 12:32 PM

  I had this strange idea come to me this morning to search my father's name on Google. What came up was this photo of him from 1956 or 1957 and a little ditty about him and the restaurant he owned placed on a USC Website.
  My father opened that restaurant and it became a USC favorite for many-many years even after he sold it. I have often wondered why there was not more about him and the restaurant on the web for, as a child, I remember it and him being discussed in magazine articles and in newspapers. What happened to those articles I do not know. And, as I was so young, I don't remember the names of the magazines and the other stuff, so I really don't even know where to search.
  My father not being more mentioned is kind of like the statement Quest Love made about the documentary he put together, *Summer of Soul,* where he stated, *"There were three hundred thousand people at that event, why can't I find any photos of it on the internet?"*
  My father and his restaurant were mentioned, all be it briefly, in a book on USC that was published a number of years back, as well. But, other than that, that's all I've seen on the internet.
  The photo of my father was a fun one. He is there making one of those faces he used to make when he and two of his customers or friends were standing over the pool table in the restaurant. Or, as he used to like to say, *"I own a beer joint."*
  Interesting, how this guy rediscovered the photo and posted it. Thanks! I'm going to leave a comment on the site. In fact, the guy really knows his USC history. In his first of two posting where he mentions my father, he says, in part, *"Does anyone remember Stubby Shaw? He opened the Trojan Barrel bar in 1955 that eventually turned into Julie's Trojan Barrel in 1975, which was not to be confused with*

Julie's Restaurant on Flower St., which was opened in 1941. Those were owned by the legendary Julie Kohl. But back to Shaw. He was a fixture to students in the 1950's and would sponsor intramural basketball teams that featured actual players like Jim Kaufman and Danny Rogers. If Shaw was well known, so was his mother. Known to dental students as "Mrs. Shaw," she was a fixture at the dental school from 1931-62. Mrs. Shaw worked with more than 3,000 dental students, the "little white haired lady who signs (the) state board examination card indicating the culmination of formal dental training. Some would say this was a time period back when USC was known for having family atmosphere."

But, back to the photograph, I think to all of the photographs I took and all of those photographs that I should've taken. I got my first semi-good 35mm camera when I was in junior high school. It was a Yashica. I was taking a photo class at the time and it was there that I learned how to develop film and all that. That's when I started seriously taking photos.

The thing was, soon after that I got really into the whole Eastern tradition of spirituality. It was always a battle between avoiding being considered materialistic and living a creative life; that sometimes involved owning material objects like cameras. So, many of the photos I should have taken I did not have my camera with me.

It's also kind of interesting, speaking of photos on the internet... I follow the Swami Satchidananda page on a few of the platforms and every now and then they post a photo of Gurudev that I took. I get it, they probably don't know that I was the one who took that photo. They just found it somewhere or got it from someone that I gave it to. And, I guess that's true art and true spirituality—taking no credit. But, it does make me feel kind of strange when a piece of history that I captured is presented and I am not mentioned.

As for that guy who posted about my father, I think that's great that he cares! ...Cares enough to post the photo and to write that piece in May of 2021.

My Yashica, long gone... I think one of my girlfriends kept it when we went our separate ways many-many years ago.

Now, everybody has a camera right in their phone. Billions of more photos are taken every day. But, digital photos are not really like physical photos. Unless you have a reason, you really are not forced to taking another look back through time.

As for my father, I've told the story before, but he sold the restaurant to two of his friends, the McKeever Brothers, that are also mentioned in the piece, with the intention of retiring young. But, retirement did not suit him so he eventually became the Food and Beverage Manager for then newly opened *Los Angeles Forum*. There he had a massive heart attack and passed away in 1968. This is all history and, of course, I have the family photos of him, but seeing a photograph that someone else took of him when he was his happiest, in his element, is a great gift.

The internet is a strange thing…

Emptiness
03/Feb/2022 09:13 AM

The Sanskrit word for emptiness is, *"Sūnyabhāva."* Meaning, a cosmic state of emptiness.

In Eastern Spiritual Traditions, it is understood that the ideal state of and for Spiritual Human Awareness is to remove all of the clutter that exists in our minds and our lives and move to a state of Divine Understanding that can only be had when one is free from the constraints of all of the things that hold us back and bound.

Have you ever watched the TV show, Hoarders? This is a television series that depicts the life of people who collect an insane amount of possessions, so much so that if they do not get rid of at least most of it something very dramatic is going to happen to their life.

Even before this show was in syndication I watched a documentary about a lady in San Francisco, who had an enormous hoard going on in her apartment. If she did not get rid of it, they were going to evict her. This woman refused to get rid of her stuff, however, and, as such, she ended up on the street. What happened to her after that, the documentary did not show. But obviously, it was not a good thing.

When you watch the show, Hoarders, you see how each of these people concocts their own unique reason for collecting a vast amount of stuff. Mostly, it is trash and junk but filtered within all of that are generally a few things of value. The one thing that all of these hoarders possess is a belief that they need all of that stuff. …That all of that stuff gives them something they are missing. …That it provides something to their life that they do not have without it. Certainly, hoarding is a psychological disfunction but in the mind of the hoarder that does not change their logic.

Universally, when any of these people are confronted with their hoarding, they each fight and refuse to let go.

Some may even see the logic and the need to clean their life space but doing it is near impossible. In fact, I am certain when the specific episode of the show is over and, at least a certain amount of their space is cleared, they go right back to hoarding.

I have known a couple of hoarders. They each pretend that what they are doing has a reason. One of the hoarders I knew was very organized in his hoarding. Everything was in boxes. But, it lined every wall of his home. Another hoarder I know attributes it to his business. In fact, at one point the fire department came in and told him he had to clean up. He did. But, what he did was to pack all of this massive amounts of equipment, in various states of disrepair, onto industrial shelves in his rear enclosed garage area which he now keeps closed off and hidden from the fire department. But, the front of his shop soon was refilled. It's really scary. It's hard to even walk in there.

As his finances are not in great shape, years ago I suggested that he take a few minutes each morning and start selling his stuff on eBay. But, he believes he may need that, *"Something,"* for some project, someday. But, will he? This is the plight of the hoarder.

This is the thing, each hoarder has a reason for their hoarding. It may sound very logical to them. But, they apparently cannot or do not want to see what the rest of the world sees. Namely, a big pile of trash and junk.

If we take this from the level of physicality to mentally, think about your own life, thing about the amount of junk that you hoard in your brain. Think about how your life has been lived: doing to get, doing to have, doing to experience, doing simply to do, thinking only to think; allowing a good portion of your life to lived only in your own mind and, at best, existing in a realm of fantasy. I'm sure you too have a logical explanation for living your life in this fashion.

Most people live in their mind and project what is in their mind out to their realms of reality. True or false, right or wrong, they cannot even truly decerning which is which. At best, it is solely defined simply by their own definition of reality, demarcated within their own process of thought.

The way most people live their life is in a constant state of collecting. They do this first based in their mind, in their realms of desire and fantasy, and then bring it outwards toward the physical plane. They do what they do to get what they want. But, when they get, do they even want it anymore?

Think about your own life. Think about your own set of desires. Think about all of the thoughts you have thought, all of the emotions you have felt. Why did you pile all of that stuff into your brain? And, did what mattered yesterday actually matter today?

Whenever I go into a thrift stores these days, I always see people with their phone in their hands looking up the values of some object that is in front of them. These people are obvious eBay resellers or maybe even swap meet resellers. I think that would be a horrible way to make a living but there they are, contemplating purchasing something that somebody else discarded in order to sell it to someone else. Possession to possession to possession; once wanted but wanted no more.

What I am saying here is, you need to very consciously consider the things you bring into your mind and your life. Yes, that something may make you feel a certain kind of way for a moment but then all it becomes is Life Junk. How much Life Junk do you really want? How much Life Junk do you really need?

As stated in the Tao Te Ching, *"To the person of the world, everyday something is gained. To the person of Tao, everyday something is lost."*

Certainly, Bob Dylan may have said it best, and it's been quoted a million times in a million places, *"When you ain't got nothing, you got nothing to lose."* But, it doesn't have to be that harsh. The thing that you need to be very conscious of is the fact that there is a limit to what possessions can provide you with—particularly possession based solely upon a projected, undefined need from your mind. There is a limit to what Mind Junk can give you. ...All that nonsense that floats around unhindered in your brain. You can live a better life. You can live in a better life space. You can think better thoughts. You can have less financial turmoil if only you stop spending on needless things that a month down the road you will not even use.

Free yourself. It's really as simple as that. Make a personal decision to meditate upon and embrace, śūnyabhāva. Just think how free your life could become if you allow it to become free. It's all in you. It's a choice only you can make. Try it. Try a little emptiness. You may find it to be amazing.

A Seller's Market
and the People Who Only Think About Themselves
02/Feb/2022 09:04 AM

  Do you ever notice that when someone is attempting to sell you something, what they have is gold? …What they have is the top of the line and is exactly what you want. But, it's all a self-projected lie. It's just another something. This is especially the case when someone approaches you. They tell you how good it is, how valuable it is, how much you need it, how it will make your life better, and maybe even how good they are. Please…

  Somebody contacted me (again) today trying to sell me their script. Whenever someone does this it is always makes me very aware of the fact that this person does not do their research—they do not know me, what I do, or what I'm about at all. They are just throwing possibilities out there in the wind.

  This, of course, is not the first time this has happened and it probably won't be the last. BAM! I deleted the email but then I had a realization that I probably should have kept all of those emails, from over all these many years, because they are all so much the same. I could have made a book out of them of something??? Oh well, too late now.

  The thing that always amuses me the most about these kind of offers, is how people hype themselves up. …What they have done and why I should pay them for their whatever. It's all the same words dreamed in a different sentence.

  I guess that's the problem with Hollywood, it's all about the promise of the dream. It's all about that one person or persons who, *"Made it,"* which gives everyone else the idea that they can make it too. It just ain't that easy.

  Hell, if I wanted to shoot a script-based movie I have several scripts that I wrote way back in the way back when that I have never produced. I could even write another one if the inclination struck me. But, that just not my art form.

I think this is where the problem (if you want to call it that) with art begins. People want to sell their art. They want other people to buy their art. But, if art is truly art should it be offered up on the auction block? Sure, it is. But, think about if this was not the reason for making art. Think how free that art would be.

There used to be this group of poets in the '50s and early '60s who would write their poetry, congregate with their crew and read it. Then, they would burn it. That's art. That's freedom.

But, everybody wants to be that something. But, that something is so illusive. That something is so abstract. I think the main thing you have to think about is if you have to hock your wares to people you don't know, at least know what they are about. You just aren't going to sell your screenplay to a guy who makes Zen Films.

Anti Shadow
01/Feb/2022 09:45 AM

Yesterday's edition of the TV Show, *Extra* devoted the entire show to their correspondent Cheslie Kryst who took her own life by jumping to her death from her apartment building in Manhattan two days ago. It was a fitting tribute that would bring tears to your eyes. It did to mine. They spoke about how positive she was and they showed clips of how she was always smiling and dancing. Very sad! Gayle King, who knew her, on her *CBS Mornings* show yesterday said an important statement, *"How can you help someone when you don't know they need help?"* That's powerful. I mean, there is all of this stuff going on in all of our minds and who really knows what is hidden within the depth of our being? I know I suffered through years of intense anxiety, (though I didn't even know that was what it was), when I was younger and I never told anybody. So, nobody knew.

But, here's the other side of the issue, sometimes you tell someone something and they just don't even care. I remember I literally had a nervous breakdown, due to all of the undefined anxiety, when I was driving my mother to the airport to pick up my aunt one day. Her only words were, *"Pull over."* She got out of my van and took a taxi to the airport, met my aunt, put her on the bus to Hollywood and then took a bus downtown to go to work, leaving me totally alone, breaking down, and fucked. I can say, *"Who would do that?"* But, I already have my answer.

Had I just been told I was suffering severe anxiety and perhaps given some tools to combat it, like I was provided with many years later, all of that pain could have been avoided. But, I was not. Just like Cheslie, I kept the pain to myself. Think across the globe, how many people are psychologically and emotionally suffering right now? How many people are doing it with a smile on their face, hiding what it really going on inside?

The tributes are still coming in for her. And, that's great! She deserves it. The sad thing is, in a week or a month, she will be forgotten by all of those who did not personally know her. And, she was famous. Now, think about what happens when you or I pass on. Who will care? Who will remember? How long will we be remember for? Probably not very long at all.

I think we each need to remove the shadows from our life. I actually call this the, *"Anti Shadow."* What it entails is consciously doing something to remove that whatever is haunting you. The Anti Shadow can really be anything. But, what it involves is doing. You have to go outside. I mean, think about something that you actually like to do. When that darkness hits you, go and do that something. Exercise is always a good thing. Ride a bike. Take a walk. If you have a friend, go out and have breakfast, lunch or dinner; grab a latte or a drink in a bar. If you're alone, don't let that stop you. The one thing is, you have to get out. You have to interact. You have to go somewhere where there are other people and something going on. Maybe you will meet someone. Say, *"Hi,"* to people as you pass by. Strike up a conversation. Go to church. Go to the mall. Go take a class. Go anywhere. Go do something where your mind will be removed from you focusing on the shadows. Even if you don't meet anyone, (and don't expect to as that may be a shadow inducing let down in itself if you don't), but get out there and do—remove that shadow; invoke the Anti Shadow.

Maybe I'll call my next music collection, Anti Shadow. Maybe I'll make it really upbeat. For those of you who follow my music, you know a lot of what I've focused on for the past several years is very droney, dark, and deep gothic, where the listener is forced to seek out the subtle musical impressions. Maybe I'll turn that around next time.

Like I suggested yesterday, *"Reach out and help someone."* Do that again today. That's a good thing. It's always a good thing. Plus, it's a GREAT thing to do if you're invoking the Anti Shadow.

If you've never suffered psychologically, good for you. You've lived an easy existence. But, a lot of us have—a lot of us still do. Sometimes those people who are suffering the most have a smile on their face and are constantly dancing. Don't let it fool you. Obviously, they may be hurting too.

If you hurt, do something to unhurt. I know, from personally experience, this can be very hard and asking for help may even be embarrassing. But, do something! Get Out.

Live the Anti Shadow.

No Good Way to Die
31/Jan/2022 08:10 AM

As we have been locked into these years of the COVID-19 Coronavirus Pandemic, we have been constantly reminded about death. Every day and every night on the news we are told of the number of people who have died.

There have been other times when death was very prevalent. In times of war or during periods of ethnic or religious cleansing, the message of death has swept over the planet and, in some cases, the true numbers of the deceased did not become known until years or decades later.

In our personal lives, we each lose those we love to the hands of death. There is just no way around that fact. It seems that the one true telling fact about this process is, however, there is no good way to die.

When a life is taken by some outward factor, there is little that can be done. In some cases, the oncoming of death can be fought off for a short amount of time by medicine and maybe even prayer, but when it finally arrives there is nothing that can keep it at bay.

Perhaps the most impactful of enacted death is brought about when someone takes their own life. Though religion tells us this is a sin, it is my belief that it is a person's choice if they no longer wish to live; that is there prerogative. But, I don't believe that most people who commit suicide really want to die, they simply want their life to be better but can find no way to make it so.

In recently times, medically induced suicide has become legal in some states when a person with a terminal illness and is experiencing unmanageable pain and other similar conditions. This seems to be a humane situation. But then, there are the people who take their own life by much more drastic measures. Those are the one's that we can't help but wonder why.

In modern culture, there are those who rise to the top of their field and still choose to end their own life. Though we most likely do not personally know these people, there death can be very personally experienced. For some, there is an obvious reason. For others, not so much. For example, when Hemingway took is own life, he had previously been involved in a couple of drastic plane crashes in Africa which left him with brain trauma. Combine that with his deepening depression and he ended up being given two extreme courses of electroshock therapy. From this, he could barely construct a sentence anymore. This, for a writer of his statue, was just too much. He took his own life. Then there are people like Kurt Cobain. The man was suffering from an array of psychological issues and addiction which lead him down the road to suicide. Though many would question why he couldn't find the help he needed, sometimes it is just not that easy for a person to find help.

People like Anthony Bourdain took his own life. There he was a chef at the top of his game, traveling the world for his show on CNN but whatever thing he was feeling, he felt it so strongly that he no longer desired to be alive. Yesterday, Cheslie Kryst threw herself from a sixty-story building in New York City. There she was, thirty years old, a stunningly beautiful woman, former Miss U.S.A., a lawyer, and a correspondent on a nation entertainment show. We all can question, *"Why?"* But, she made her choice.

Then, there are people like Owen Wilson; literally a movie star and he attempted to commit suicide. He was found and his death prevented, however. But again, the question of, *"Why,"* is raised.

In life, we each live in our state of mental reality. In life, we each encounter our own levels of pain. What hurts one person internally may not affect another. Knowing this, you should never judge what a person is feeling or why they are feeling it and you should never dismiss a person's feeling. You should simply accept the fact that is what they are experiencing and if something is hurting them you should do all that you can to guide them to a better place in a positive manner. Never negate their feelings.

Life is not easy. Even for those who seem to be at the top of the world and have everything. They too feel what they feel. They too experience life the way they experience life and they do so in their own unique manner.

Think to a time when you were hurting. No matter what the cause, that was what you were feeling. Maybe someone understood your pain and tried to help you. Maybe no one understood your pain and maybe even told you to stop feeling it. In either case, that was what you were felling which is what caused you to guide your life actions. In some cases, these feelings take a person down a dark road and that is sad because that can lead to a person taking their own life. But, if you know a person who is hurting and you either helped in the creation of that pain or did nothing to remedy that pain, who is truly at fault?

In life, your one true mission should be to help everyone you can. In life, your personal objective should be to help the people you personally know and those you do not know. Because if you are not helping, if you are not spreading goodness everywhere you go, than what are you actually doing?

Like I say over and over again, all life begins with you. Which also mean, all death begins with you. What you do not only affects you but it has the potential to spread out and affect many-many more people. Again, your life should be about helping.

Today, why don't we do an exercise? Let's go out an help somebody. If you know someone that is hurting go and give them a hand. Do something that will make that hurt go away, even if just for a moment. If you do not personally know someone that is in pain, go out and help someone else. Take the time to find someone and give them something that makes their life just a little bit better.

We all need to get the focus of our life out of our own head and care enough to help someone else. Do this and it has the potential to change everything. Maybe a person will live instead of die.

Things Used to Be a Lot More Free
30/Jan/2022 10:31 AM

I used to go outside and jump on my motorcycle and just take off. It was a great feeling. Just turned the key, kick start it, and I was on my way. No helmet required. It was just free.

Of course, I got hit by a car one day. My skull got fractured in numerous places, had to have brain surgery, several bones were broken, cartilage and muscles ripped and torn, and my life was never the same. But, I remember the freedom that once was but is there no more.

I remember the days when you didn't have to wear seatbelts in your car. You would just jump in and drive off. In fact, my '64 356, didn't even have seat beats. They weren't issued with that car. Here in Cali, if your car was manufactured before a certain date, they couldn't give you a ticket for not wearing them. Just so much freer. Though, I get it, not near a safe. Now, don't wear 'em and you get a ticket. I remember the time I got my first no seatbelt ticket. I was on my way to the NAMM show and the law had just gone into effect. This cop pulled me over and was just such a dick. Just not worth it. Now, I always put mine on. But, not near as free.

I remember the first time I spent any real time in Texas. I was asked to go down there and do a movie. One of the first things I noticed was that in all of the gas stations, and places like that, they had this pile of one-off beers in a large bucket of ice. People would come in a get gas or whatever and grab themselves a beer for the road. I thought that was so cool. It was all just there for the taking. Garb a beer and go. How free was that? Then, times changed and the drunk driving laws all got so much more severe. Good thing, I guess. But, I always thought it was a little too tight when they decided that you could get busted for drinking even one beer. Just no freedom left.

It seems like everything is getting so much less free. Really… Think about it. Think of all the rules telling you all the things that you just can't do anymore. They just seem to be growing and growing and growing and growing. I don't know? Is that making the world any better? What I do know is that there is the experience of so much lack of freedom. Freedom that was once there but is there no more.

I don't know? Where can you feel freedom anymore?

Standing Up for What You Believe
28/Jan/2022 04:15 PM

One of the big news stories of the week was Neil Young told Spotify to choose him or Joe Rogan due to the fact that he believes Joe Rogan's negative stance on the COVID-19 Coronavirus vaccine and the misinformation he is disseminating has the potential to kill people.

I've never listened to Joe Rogan's podcast. In fact, I've never listened to anybody's podcast. I'm just too busy getting things done to care about a person's blibber-blabber.

But, of course, Spotify choose Rogan. I think we all saw that one coming a mile away. I mean, think about it, Neil Young is old, most of the Gen Z generation and a lot of Millennials probably don't even know who or what he is.

Now, I will say, I'm on Team Neil Young here all the way. Like I was saying to my lady today when we were having lunch and we were discussing the people who refuse to get the vaccine, *"People choose what they are told is the pathway of god because of what their minister (or people like Rogan) has to say and they don't get the vaccine, yet when they are there in the ICU dying from COVID because they didn't get the vaccine they are praying to god asking for him (or her) to save them and asking, why me?"* The answer is, you didn't get vaccinated.

But, I get it, everybody has their opinion and makes their own choices even if their choices may kill them. I also get why Spotify choose Joe Rogan over Neil Young; money.

But, the point of all this is, Neil Young stood up for what he believed. He took a stance and put his own livelihood on the line in doing so. Most people when they don't like something someone is saying or doing just do things like throw shots at them; criticize them and try to hurt them from afar. That is very cowardly. Neil Young stepped up to the plate and made a stand-by doing something he could control. He created that music. That was something positive in and of itself. As he created it, he choose to take control over and take it down from a platform that he believes was doing harm to people in what else they were offering.

I think you need to think about this. I think you need to think about this when you take a stand. Sure, you can easily attack someone by saying negative things about them but what horse do you have in that race? That's just you telling other people what you think and feel. Maybe you are right, maybe you are wrong, but if all you do is attack by throwing nothing meaningful of your own into the pot then what do your words of attack actually mean? How have you proven your commitment to the fight? What do your actions mean if there is nothing that you stand to lose?

You can make your own decisions in life. I've had people that were close to me die from COVID-19, pre the wide availability of the vaccine, so I know what COVID-19 can do. I'm pro vax. But, more than that, and on the larger scale of life, we hear people demeaning, criticizing, and attacking people all the time, (maybe you do it too), but if you are not willing to fight the battle with something that is important to you than who actually wins and who actually losses in any bout of the Rock'em Sock'em Robots?

Mopping Up Your Mess on the Road to Peace
28/Jan/2022 07:52 AM

Back in the '90, I used to live in this apartment in Redondo. At night, every now and then, you could hear the sound of a train passing by. The thing is, the nearest train tracks were miles away. Somehow, by some means, the sound of the train traveled over land and found its way to our ears.

Back in the 1970s, when CB radios were all the rage, every now and then you would get a skip. The thing is, the radio waves of a CB only travel a relatively short distance but every now and then, if the clouds in the sky were just right, causing the radio waves to bounce, you could talk to someone many-many miles away. The other CBer commonly didn't initially believe they were speaking to someone at that distance. But, the proof was the proof.

Back when I was in high school, I used to like to put on my headphone when I went to bed. You know those big bulky contraptions from the '70s. I used to lay there in the dark, turn the dial, and every now and then I could get this radio station from Monterey, California. Now, Monterey is about four hundred miles from Hollywood, so this made me, as a teenager, quite excited. The music was the same but my ability to get it from a place so far away set all kinds of happiness into motion.

What does all this tell us? It tells us, what you do has the potential to travel. You may not expect what you do to travel, you may have no intention of it traveling, but what you say and what you do has the potential to travel very far, affecting many things and many people. Knowing this, you must really contemplate what you do before you do it because it could have lasting impressions.

I suppose I could finish this piece with that last sentence but to peer just a bit deeper into this subject… When you look to the life of most people, they live a simple existence. They are born, they go to school, they go to work, they have a family, and they die. For some, they live a good and calm existence, based upon their own personality and their choice of life mates. For others, they pass through their existence in a much more turbulent manner. Also defined by their personality and their choice of life mates. But, the fact of the fact is, who do you believe lives a better life? The calm, passive individual or the one who constantly causes a stir? Which one are you?

If you turn this around slightly, think about the people you've encountered. Whether they be family or friends or simply passing people on the road of life; which one's did you prefer to interact with? My guess would be, the answer is obvious: the calm, the good, and the peaceful.

Many people create a mess in life. They create a mess in their own life and, from this, they go outwards and create a mess in the life of other people. Think about a time when someone created a mess in your life. Bring to mind a time when you created a mess in the life of someone else. No matter anyone's motivation, a mess is what was created. And, a mess is never pretty or peace creating.

What did you do to mop up any mess you created in the life of that someone else? What did that someone else do to mop up the mess they created in your life? If nothing was done, nothing was done, and what was done has continued to span outwards since it was done. It has continued to move farther and farther out to the outer banks. As it was never undone, it remains forever done. Thus, its capacity to alter life, in a negative manner, lives on forever. Is that they way things should be? Is that the way you should be?

Again, looking to the life of most people, they live a simple existence. They live, they survive, they pass through their time in life, they die. They come and then they go. That's the law of life. With such things as Reality TV, the definition of life has changed somewhat. It has put a new poison in the pill. People have become rich and famous for doing nothing. And, this is alluring to those with a certain mindset. Hand-in-hand with this, many of the actions portrayed on these shows are less than good, helpful, and harmless. Controversy breeds viewership which projects a way of behavior that provides people of a certain mindset with a false projection of the way life should be lived.

How often do you study and take account of your actions? How often do you care how what you are saying or what you are doing to someone or something will only affect them in a positive manner? If you love them you care. If you don't, you don't, and it is just the opposite. But, every sound you project out into the ethos has the potential to reverberate forever and forever. If that reverberation is based in negativity, on any level, no matter what your self-defined justification may be, all it creates is an environment of everlasting negativity which then becomes the definition of your life.

All things emanate from one source.

In life, you have a few choices to make. The first being, what are you going to do? The second being, what are you going to do about what you have done?

If you can't be whole and pure enough to embrace the simplicity of peace and simple do-goodness, then what will reverberate from you?

If you question this question, before you ever do or say anything negative, ask yourself, would you want someone to do to you what you are about to do to someone else?

In life, if you wish to live a peaceful and good life, think before you do and if what you do does something negative, mop up your mess. It's really as simple as that.

Those Who Can Do
27/Jan/2022 07:36 AM

Life is an interplay of desire, projection, interaction, failure, and success. A person can only achieve what they have the ability to achieve. Like the only saying goes, *"Those who can do. Those who can't teach."* But, I feel that adage is a bit harsh. Think about it, teaching is one of the highest professions there is. It is a person caring enough to learn the rules and the techniques and then share their developed knowledge with others. It takes an advanced university degree if a person wants to be a teacher. That is an accomplishment in and of itself. That takes desire, focus, and dedication which is something that few people possess. I believe the more appropriate statement should be, *"Those who can do. Those who can't review."* Because it's very easy to possess an option. It is very hard to have a vision and bring it into reality.

The question(s) you must ask yourself each day are: *"What am I doing to do? What am I doing to create the life and the lifestyle I desire? What am I doing to shape any creation I have in my mind and make it a reality?"*

Everybody desires a different something. We are each shaped by the factors that formed our life and the situations that surround us. But, how much control do you take over any of that? How much focus do you focus on reaching your end goal? Everybody wants to be a Superhero. Though everyone wants this, what are you doing to achieve this? To reach Superhero status takes drive, desire, ego, (believing you are good enough), and for some lies. Lies they tell themselves and lies they tell to others. But, for those who reach this plateau, with very few exceptions, how they get there is by their doing. What are you doing to reach the place in life where you dream of dwelling?

From a metaphysical perspective, the problem with most people's doing is they do with only themselves in focus. They do for only themselves. They do to get what they want and they could care less about anyone else. Though this is the common pathway of reality, if you do your do by doing it that way, all you create is a lot of animosity and hard feelings. Now, admittedly, most people don't care. If they have achieved any small portion of what they want that is all that matters. But, here comes the problem, if that is how you behave, sooner or later that becomes the definition of all you have gained. Thus, no longer will you be viewed as a person who truly achieved but simply as a scoundrel. Some people don't care. They got what they got and that's good enough for them. But, if you don't care, all that you got will never remain. That's just the way it works.

    The thing is, if you want to become that Superhero, you must possess the focus to work towards it. But, you should also care about the pathway that you take and those who are walking hand-in-hand with you. If you don't, then you don't. But, then what?

Things You Don't Want to Know
26/Jan/2022 08:00 AM

In Sanskrit, the word for knowing is, *"Anubhāvin."* The term for not knowing is, *"Adṛṣṭa."* Do you ever think about how in life there are certain things that you would just prefer not to know—there are things you wish you didn't know?

Think about a time when you believed what you believed about a person or about a situation. Then, some truth was revealed to you and once you heard it that truth broke your heart. No longer could you ever view that person or that thing in the same way. I believe we have all experienced those moments in our lives. Those instantaneous flashes where everything was previously fine and then it was not. Did you really want to know that knowledge?

On the pathway of rising human consciousness, it is always believed that the veils must be removed—that the truth must be presented. But, as true as that may be for the things that don't really matter in some very personal way, there is this whole other level of life experience where living in a state of non-knowing may be best.

Certainly, the truth is the truth is the truth and that is the truth. No matter how much someone hides that truth that does not change the truth. But, not knowing also does not change that truth, it simply remains in the space of abstract oblivion.

People in relationships often push to hear the truth of their friend's or their partner's past. They push to know, but once they know, that knowledge can never be forgotten. Not forgotten it can never be overlooked. Thus, by knowing there is never the un-knowing; forever that person is defined by what you know.

Think about a, *"Somebody,"* in your life. Think about a person that once-upon-a-time you felt one way about them, but then, as you came to know them better, you redefined your feelings. Think about the moment you found out that something about them that changed how you felt about them. Did that new-knowledge change who that person actually was or did it simply redefine them in your brain?

Here's the thing, just because you find out some deep dark secret about a person, just because you come to hold some new knowledge about somebody's something, that never changes who they are. In fact, just because you think you know does not mean you truly know as all knowledge is simply defined by individual definitions within a person's own psyche. ...You define life one way, another person may define it very differently.

This is where the fact of knowledge becomes quite complex, particularly when it is in relation to another person. You know what you know about them. But, all you know is simply something you think you know. All you know is something that is only defined in your own mind. Your definitions of a person's suchness are only your definitions. What you think about a person is only defined by your own mind. This is why judgement of someone/anyone is only done by the most feeble minded. As, at best, all they are doing is casting a personal definition onto the life of someone else.

Think about it... You find something out about a person, something that you did not previously know. That something change how you view them. But, think about all of the other things that you do not know. Ponder all of the levels of their reality that could still be revealed.

Knowing is knowing but knowing is only as good as what you know. ...Knowing is only as good as how you define what you have found out.

The truth in the knowing leads us to understand that no one can truly know anyone or anything, at best all they can do is find a set of parameters in which to judge them based upon their own personal system of belief.

So, next time you believe you know someone or something, think again. At best, all you are doing is casting your judgement onto who you believe that somebody or that something to be. Is that true knowledge? The obvious answer is, no.

Next time you think you know, know that you don't know.

Buying a Car During the Pandemic or NOT
25/Jan/2022 04:08 PM

    I recently mentioned in this blog that I still have not purchased another car since my car got totaled like three months ago. I received several questions of why not. Thanks for the asking but let me tell you what's going on…

    Just today, I saw a car being offered by a dealer online. I gave the dealership a call. Here's what they told me. You take the base price of the car, then they add $3,000.00 on to it. *"Why,"* I ask. No answer. Meaning, they do it just because they can. Then, they add $2,500.00 onto the price of the car because they want to add one of those alarm system that they, the powers that be, can use to track you down and shut down the car. I had heard about that on the news. Some dealerships are doing that because when people miss their payments and they want to repo the car it makes it way easier for them to find it. I tell the salesman, (well actually a saleswoman), *"I'm going to pay cash." "That doesn't matter. We don't sell cars without that feature."* What! Then, she tells me, they add on $450.00 for tires. Are you kidding me! Don't cars come from the factory with tires? There was also about another $1,000.00 of incidental additives that had no reason and some other money add-ons as well. My quick calculation was that the car would cost about $6,000.00 over MSRP. Are you kidding me!

    Then, comes the kicker. The car they had advertised and I called about was not even on the lot yet. It was in transit. Unbelievable…

    PS: This was not the first time I encountered this style of price gouging trying to find a car.

    I don't know if you have ever bought a new car in the past, but the salespeople would offer you discounts just so you would buy the car from their dealership. Obviously, no more. So, I don't know what I'm going to do? I thought when my car got totaled it was some secret gift from the great beyond causing me to move forward in my life. I guess it was just some inconsiderate asshole fucking with my life.

It's kind of like this funny moment that I included at the end of documentary I did about Donald G. Jackson, *Diary of a Michigan Migrant Film Worker.* He passionately exclaims, so-and-so says, *"Everything happens for a reason. I think sometimes that reason is just to FUCK you over!"*

…Just think, if some savvy car manufacture would step back into the old school and make a car using only American parts that don't have to be imported and no computer chips that are now in short supply they could be making a killing. Make a real car with American Steel.

Anyway… So, to answer your questions, that's what's going on. That's why I haven't bought another car.

So, if any of you people out there in Internetland have a line on one, new or used, and don't want to charge me an extra $6,000.00 just because you can, let me know.

*   *   *

25/Jan/2022 11:30 AM

You can drop your letter in any mailbox but if you don't put an address on it the letter will never get to who you wrote it for.

Interpreting Your Reality
25/Jan/2022 07:45 AM

    Have you ever had the situation where you lived through an experience and you felt a certain way about that experience but as time went on you begin to understand that life-event differently and you came to a new and different conclusion about what took place?

    Have you ever lived a life-event and when you told people about it you described it somewhat differently to the various people you spoke with; defined by who that other person was?

    Life/your life is defined by your interpretation of what events you live. Two or more people may live through the exact experience but they each will define, interpret, and portray that experience completely differently.

    When you are living through your life experiences do you ever step back from them and calculate how you are actually feeling about them and how, once that experience is over, you will actually define that experience?

    I was watching the new documentary on A&E last night about Hugh Hefner and his Playboy empire. Though they threw in a few positive comments, presented by some of his well-wishers, the piece was obviously a hatchet job. They are trying to #cancel him postmortem.

    Now, I have no feeling about the man one way or the other. I never met him. The few times I was invited to one of his wild parties at the Playboy Mansion I never attended. That's just not me. Though I knew several women who did attend those events. But, we all knew who and what he was about and what he stood for. Did he help to orchestrate a change in the modern mindset of the Western world? Probably. He did what he did based in his definition of pushing the boundaries of human existence in the direction he wanted by living a life defined by his interpretation of excess.

He died just a few years ago. Times have changed even since that relatively recent point in history. This doc focuses on this new mindset that has emerged.

In my lifetime, I have watched how at one point in history sexual morays fell away and now those walls are being rebuilt. Good or bad that is open to individual interpretation.

It is not that Hef and his empire did not always have its critics. But, in this doc they focus on the people that were close to him. Many of the woman, one in particular, rose to relative wealth and fame due to her relationship with Hefner. She used to praise him, now she is a harsh critic. Did her life change? Did her experience(s) change? Or, did she simply alter her interception of her experience(s)? ...Is she simply following the trends of the time to once again capitalize on knowing the man?

This is the thing about documentaries, biographies, or simply discussions that take place while sitting at a bar or around the dinner table, all things are defined by the focus of the interpretation. With this/from this, though individual beliefs and understandings may be presented, all of these discourses are presented from an outside perspective. In this case of this documentary, the man, himself, is no longer alive so he cannot speak, *"His truth."* This is why I always find this style of documentation disingenuous. How can you talk about a man when he is no longer alive? How can you attack him when he is not available to defend himself?

Many people in this documentary complained about how Hef was in control and was the all-powerful individual guiding his empire. These people speak as if this is something bad or wrong. It immediately made me state, *"Every job is like that!"* For anyone out there who has ever had a job, you will agree. There is always the boss who tells you what to do. Maybe that boss is nice, maybe that boss is a jerk, maybe you love your job, maybe you hate it, but, at any job, there is always that someone in control and, if you are simply an employee, that person is not you. That's just life!

If you ever watched the Hefner reality show, *"The Girls Next Door,"* you already heard and witnessed how Hef behaved. If you watch this new doc what you see is new interpretations about that behavior. Was he any different? No. Where these girls that they interviewed for this doc any different? I don't know? Or, did they simply change their interpretations of their life-events? But, the question that has to be asked is, why?

As you pass through life, it is essential that you take stock of what is going on in your life. It is imperative that you really live your life events for those events are all you have to define your life. If you change your definition of your lived life events, that is your prerogative, but if you do change the way you tell your story, simply defined by whom you are telling it to, what does that say about your truth?

Everyone should be able to live a good life. I wish everybody had that chance. The main focus of part two of this documentary was a woman who came to L.A., with stars in her eyes, and made her living as waitress. Hefner took her away from that lifestyle and provided her with that ticket to the stars that she desired. But, she didn't have to make that choice? She could have said, *"No,"* and remained a waitress but she did not. Now, again, here she is rising to notoriety by speaking (negatively) about the man and the empire that provided her with that passageway to fame. Is that right? I don't know? I guess that's up to each person. But, you really need to consider does the truth of any experience actually change simply by the way a person interpolates it? If it does, that means there is no absolute truth to your lived reality.

* * *
24/Jan/2022 01:23 PM

How often do you listen to yourself walk?

How often do you question what is the impact your steps are having on the world around you?

* * *
24/Jan/2022 08:35 AM

When there's no requirement what are the requirements?

* * *
24/Jan/2022 07:18 AM

If you could erase all of your mistakes and your embarrassments what would your life become?

If you could erase all of the pain you caused to anyone else what would your life become?

Someone Else's Truth
24/Jan/2022 07:03 AM

  The story I'm about to tell you here may be better left to one of my poems or one of my novels. In fact, maybe it already was cast to some form of literature. ...I've written so many poems, short stories, novellas, novels, and the like that sometimes I forget which tales I have told. All this being said, here it goes... You may find it interesting and/or helpful.

  I went into my local Banana Republic back in the late '80s. I used to love Banana Republic. For those of you of a different time and space in history you probably don't know this but BR used to be very different from what it has evolved into in this period of time. Back in the day, they were all about the khaki/safari style clothing but done with a high-end flare. Their stores had actual jeeps on a rocky landscape in their front windows. And, what they offered was just very-very trend setting for the era. In fact, I think my favorite sport coat of all time I purchased at that store. It was this khaki blazer with elbow patches... I don't know? It was just very cool. I loved it. But, before I get too far off track...

  This one evening I went in there. Just one of those times when you go shopping for no good reason. In the store this beautiful young African-American woman came up to help me. It seemed that we had instant chemistry. At the time, I was very actively single. I gave her my number, she gave me hers, and a few days later we were out on a date.

  The evening of the date, I went to pick her up at the apartment she lived in with her mother. Her mother was this seemingly nice lady with a thick Jamaican accent. At the time, it seemed kind of weird to have to meet a mother on a first date. But, whatever...

  This girl was obviously very tuned into what was going on. Very mature, though I assumed she was younger than me. I asked her what she wanted to do and, as it turned out, she wanted to see this art-house film that was only showing in Century City. Fine with me.

We drove there in my Porsche. We walked holding hands, saw the movie, and all was well with the world. After that, we went to the beach to take a nighttime walk. This girl was all over me. I mean, she was coming at me hard. She wanted me to take her back to my apartment with one intention in mind. Though I was more than willing, something just seemed off. For some reason, I asked her how old she was. She (honestly) told me she was seventeen. She was still in high school. Wow! That ended that. You know, and I'll speak more about this in a moment, but legal is legal and that hook up would have been illegal. I hold a certain morality and, as such, I took this sweet young girl home, to her home.

Now, I get it, when you are a teenager you feel like an adult. I know by the time I was seventeen I thought I was. Most of my friends were thirty or so. Whenever they came up with the idea to take off for the nude hot springs in the high desert, I was with them. There, all the hippies and the holies smoked weed, dropped acid, or meditated. We would commune with nature while getting way too sun burn in all the places that it did not feel too good. ...I would hop in my car and take off for San Francisco, Old Mexico, or Canada at a moment's notice, leaving high school behind. Many a night, I would hang out in the last remaining coffee house in L.A. at the time, *Déjà vu* off of Hollywood Blvd., late into the late night. So, I get it. Seventeen, you feel like an adult. But, legal is legal. The fact of the matter is, however, that is not even the point to the tale I am telling.

Shortly after our date, I started getting messages left on my answering machine by this girl about how now she was a few months along. That's great, I thought, but I had nothing to do with it. Why was she calling me? The calls continued, even getting to the point where a child had apparently been born and she was telling me what she had named it and that I should come and see it. I realized that she was saying all of these words for the ears of someone else. My guess is, and it's only a guess, someone had gotten her pregnant but he took off or??? She needed a baby daddy, which is why she was so directed in trying to hook up with me. There I was, a marginally established youngish guy. I was probably twenty-nine or something. And, she figured if we hooked up, she could then tell me the baby was mine.

Now, I felt for this girl. Having a baby as a teenager cannot be easy. I knew a few girls who got pregnant when we were in high school. They went off to have their baby and I never saw them again. It can't be easy. It especially can't be easy if there is no daddy figure around.

But, more to the point, here was this beautiful young girl, cast to a world where she was living a lie. At least she was living a lie in that she was projecting some falsehood to the ears of other people, most probably her mother, for some self-conceived logic, known only to her. But, it was a lie nonetheless.

This is the thing about life, people lie. People tell stories that are created for the eyes and the ears of someone else. They create fabrication for whatever reason. But, whatever the reason, what they are speaking is not the truth. I think this is why this life incident has always remained in mind all these years. Had things been just a little bit different or had I made another decision, her life, my life, and that baby's life would have been total altered. More to the point, had she made another life decision, prior to getting pregnant, her life would have evolved on a completely different trajectory. It would not have had to be based upon a lie. And, that's the thing about lying, no matter why you are doing it, a lie is not the truth.

I've written about this previously and for those of you who read this blog you know the story. This guy, in his junky old Ford pickup, sideswiped my car, totaling it, maybe three months ago now. A week or so later I get this very articulate handwritten letter from the guy presenting a complete fabrication of what occurred. It was totally composed for the eyes of someone else. He even said he was going to take me to court and I would be the one lying to the judge if I didn't agree with the falsehoods he was presenting. Wow. All this made me smile, in that kinda/sorta sort of way because the fact was, his junky truck could drive away while my car was dead in the water. Plus, due to all the pandemic craziness and the insane prices and in-availability of cars right now, I still haven't been able to get a new car but did he even think about that? Nope. Did he care about me and my situation that he created by his erratic driving? Nope. All he thought about was fabricating a lie to try to protect himself from an accident he causes that would not have occurred had he not been driving illegally down the wrong side of the road. Like I said when I have referenced this incident previously, thank god I took photos of the accident. But, think how common that type of mendacious behavior is. Think how many people tell lies to protect their own ass every day.

    Anyway… This is the thing, people present their false narratives all the time. People tell their untruthful tales all the time. Then, in some cases, other people believe these stories. But, what are you believing if what you are told is not the truth? Moreover, what about the people who are speaking the lie? What is the truth in their life? Do they even know it? Do they even care? For example, what if I had hooked up with that girl? What if I believed I was the baby daddy? Would that have made it true? No. Yet, think how many people, all across the globe, are told lies everyday that they believe and that lie shapes their entire life. From this, they live their life based on a lie. From this, what becomes the meaning of their life? Answer: A lie. And, what becomes the meaning of the life of the liar who set the untruth into motion?

This is really something to think about every time you hear the words spoken by someone else and every time you choose to say something that is not based in the truth. You can really set a whole course of life events into motion every time you say anything. And, no matter what your motivation, if you are speaking a lie, it never becomes the truth.

As for the young lady, I don't know whatever became of her or her baby. The phone calls finally stopped. As strange as this situation was, I always wished them the best. But, the truth of the truth is, a lie never becomes the truth no matter what your reason for speaking it is. And remember, a lie can truly alter your life and the life of someone else in a negative manner. Think about it…

* * *

23/Jan/2022 09:15 AM

Nothing bad ever equals anything good.

Think about this before you make your next decision.

The Monologue Game
23/Jan/2022 04:37 AM

For anyone who has ever dabbled in acting or is, in fact, a professional actor, they will immediately confirm that doing monologues are one of the key components in training, practice, and character actualization. Basically, for those of you out there who may not be familiar with the term, a monologue is a character going into an extended dialogue about one thing or another. Generally, a monologue is focused on some in depth aspect of the character the actor is portraying.

As a filmmaker, particularly in my later character-driven films, I commonly have one or more of the characters preform a monologue in order to add depth to the storyline and/or their character. As I am an improv-based filmmaker, I choose one or more of the cast members, give them some of the basics about what I want them to talk about, let them think about it, practice and whatever, and then on the day of filming let them do what they do. This has worked better with some actors rather than others. In some cases, once the actor had finished their piece, I would feel it needed a little something more and I would suggest they continue in the same vein. For some, they run with it. For others, not so much. The problem for those who could and/or cannot effectively do this is based in the fact that what they had done is to follow the path of traditional acting and they only memorized and practiced a very specific group of words, which they spoke to the best of their ability. But, ask them to take the character monologue further and they can't do it.

I remember maybe five or so years ago this agent had contacted me in regard to possibly representing me. I was a bit skeptical, but I agreed to the meet. When we spoke on the telephone prior to meeting, she asked me to prepare a monologue which I completely dismissed. I almost thought it was a joke. I mean, you can either act or you can't. And, me spitting out some memorized Shakespeare or someone else's composed character bullshit isn't going to change who or what I am. Anyway, I go to the meeting. We talk. Then, she asks me to preform. She asked for the title of the monologue. I told her, *"I don't do those but I can spit out some improv for you if you want. Give me a subject."* But, I saw then it just was not going to work between her and I. Did she even know who and/or what I am?

Anyway, I said, *"No,"* to the representation. She went out of business a short time later so I guess that was a good choice. But, it all leads to the point of all of this. Monologues are, at least by tradition, a preconceived dialectic references to life. And, people memorize them. Then, they speak them over and over and over again throughout their life with little change.

Now, don't get me wrong, I think playing The Monologue Game can be useful and it can help to kept one's acting chops up. But, for other than acting it can also become an ongoing useless life endeavor.

Funny story… I think back to this place I was living at maybe twenty years ago or so. I was going to do this film and I wanted to get into character, just to feel who and what this guy was. So, I was playing The Monologue Game with my lady and I was going on and on about whatever. I was playing the kind of, *"I'm right. You're wrong. You're to blame,"* role. Anyway, this neighbor apparently heard me and the next day I bumped into him in the elevator where he made some snide comment about what I had been saying not realizing that I was acting. I guess that was good as I was convincing but a certain part of me really wanted to tell him, *"Fuck off and mind your own business."* But, I guess my role proved to be believable. Isn't that was acting is all about?

Another funny thing that happened to me on one of my sets was that I had the female lead going into a monologue to establish her character. Something I didn't know about the cameraman initially was, he had narcolepsy.

Anyway, the girl was doing her monologue. My eyes where on her observing her performance. All of sudden, I hear snoring in my ear. The cameraman had fallen asleep. I was beside myself. I could not stop laughing. The actress, however, was very insulted as she was so serious about her role. But, that situation made me realize that this is so much about how life actually is. People are out there speaking their truth but no one cares. They fall asleep.

In another on-camera situation, I was doing this monologue as we were driving through Hollywood at night. I drew from some of my own youthful experiences, as that is what acting is, finding that place in you that becomes the character. I was talking, I get near the end of the piece and my co-star, who was also an experienced actor, says, *"What? Huh? Did you say something?"* Again, that was such a perfect depiction about how certain people react to what is spoken to them. People say things that they wish are heard, they say them to people who they want to understand them and know the way they feel. But, how often do you tell someone something and they could care less? You express your emotions yet they do not hear a word you have said?

Here's the thing, monologues can be fun. They can be theatrical. They can be a practice-based tool in an actor's arsenal. I play The Monologue Game for fun a lot. But, whether what you are saying is something you are expressing as a means of conveying the emotions of a fictional character or as a means to express your true self, you really must be prepared to understand that no matter how many times you repeat the same monologue some people simply are not going to hear you. Maybe better put, they are so self-involved that they do not care enough to care about what you are feeling equaling what you have to say.

Think about your own life… How commonly do you truly hear what someone has to say? Do you actually listen? Do you care about everyone or only those you genuinely care about? Or, do you not really care about anyone but yourself and what you are feeling, equaling what you are monologuing about? I can tell you that you should listen, I can say you should care but is that monologue going to fall on deaf ears?

We all want people to hear what we have to say. Sometime we repeat it over and over again. We all want people to care about who we are and what we are feeling. But, face facts, some just don't. That's not right but that is the way it is. Don't be that person!

So, you can play The Monologue Game if you want. You can say the same thing over and over and over again if that is how you want to fill your life-time. You can do the same monologue to everyone you meet. But, if the person/any person doesn't care enough to hear what you have to say, what do all of those words actually come to mean?

* * *
22/Jan/2022 05:01 PM

What are you required to give?

* * *
22/Jan/2022 07:11 AM

If you are sent a message that you never receive was that message ever really sent?

* * *
21/Jan/2022 01:44 PM

If who you are was given to you by someone else, it can always be taken away.

* * *
21/Jan/2022 11:25 AM

How many people have died today?

And, how much do you care?

It's Never Going to Turn Out the Way You Thought it was Going to Turn Out
20/Jan/2022 02:55 PM

Have you ever set about on the path of creating something? If you have, you will know, that, *"Something,"* was first envisioned in your mind. Maybe you saw it so clearly. You knew what it should become. What it should look like. How it should feel. Maybe you even calculated how others would appreciate it. Did you set about to create that something? If you did, almost universally you will understand that it most probably did not turn out the way you had envisioned. That's just life. That's just creativity. That's just the way it is.

Some people have a million visions in their mind. They want to create this, they want to create that. But, a vision in the mind is not actually bringing something into reality. It's just lost to being locked into your mind.

A million people have a billion ideas; how many of them are ever brought to life? Very few. Many simply do not know how to project that mental vision into physically reality. The fact is, it's hard. It's not easy. It's easy to envision things in your mind but to bring those things into reality requires so much focus, so much effort, and oftentimes the help of other people, which brings a whole new set of undefined criteria into making what's in your mind a reality.

For anyone who has walked down the road of bringing a mental vision into physical form, they will understand, it rarely becomes ideally what was seen in your mind. For good or for bad that is the truth.

In someway, I believe this may be better. Because what's created solely in someone's mind is just theirs. It is no one else's. But, life and reality, and other people, and all the stuff you can never plan for has the ability to guide that creation down a road that was most probably never your intention.

For myself, I have spent my entire life trying to bring the creative vision that is in my mind into reality. And, I can tell you, nothing has ever become what I saw in my mind. It took on its own shape and its own form. Though I thought the thought which set the creation into motion, I long ago realized that you cannot try to force your mental vision onto reality as all that does is cause conflict.

I have watched so many people allow their mental vision to be lost because though they started to create that idea and bring it into physical form, they ran into conflict, they ran into obstacles, they ran into reality. And, not being willing to allow the reality of the reality to reform their vision, they choose to shut it down instead of forging on. What occurred? Nothing. Nothing was created. Nothing new was presented to reality.

What does this tell us? It tells us, if you hope to be a vessel for creativity, you have to be willing to allow any creative vision that you hold in your mind to ultimately be molded by whatever reality defines it. If not, you will create nothing and that which was first seen in your mind's eye will never find its way to be experienced by anyone else.

* * *
18/Jan/2022 01:12 PM

Just because you think somebody is going to do something does not mean that they are going to do it.

The Diminishing Peak Experience
17/Jan/2022 09:21 AM

For anyone who has walked down the Spiritual Path, they understand that the Peak Experience is a by-product of that journey. But, just what is the Peak Experience? In brief, it is one of those moments where all things align and your mind and your body move to a level of new peace, joy, and cosmic understanding. It may exist for only a moment in time but in that short time period all is as it should be.

A common name for the Peak Experience in Japanese is, *"Satori."* This term describes momentary and instantaneous enlightenment.

In Hinduism, enlightenment or, *"Samadhi,"* is broken up into several categories defining the various level of Samadhi. In brief, these levels are: Savikalpa Samadhi, Nirvikalpa Samadhi, Dharmamegha Samadhi, and Sahaja Samadhi. But, as in all things based in Hinduism, this categorization makes the understanding very complicated.

Whether you walk on the Spiritual Path or not, have you ever experienced one of those moments where everything just feels so awe inspired and perfect? Commonly, these occurrences occur, much more commonly and freely when you are young. This is a time space where life is new and your mind has not become confined by programming and expected expectations.

Certainly, love has the potential to drive one towards a Peak Experience. When love is felt, and especially when it is returned, there is that grand feeling of all-right-ness.

Though love may be used as an example of the feeling of the Peak Experience, the Peak Experience itself does not need to be motivated or instigated by any one event. …Though it may be. The Peak Experience simply comes over you, and in that moment of knowing, one feels the grand glory of goodness and perfection that can be experienced in life. But, almost as soon as it arrives, the Peak Experience dissipates.

The problem with the Peak Experience, (if you want to refer to it as a problem), is that once it is felt, it is known, and from this, the Feel-er hopes to feel it again. Like a drug invoking the perfect experience, it too can become an addictive focus.

In some schools of spiritual practice, they discourage people from seeking out the Peak Experience. Or, when it is felt, the zealot is taught to rebuke it. But, what it is the fun in that? So much of life is held back by the reality of living in reality that when goodness arrives, via any flavor, don't you think it should be embraced and relished?

Think about a time in your life when you had one of those experiences—that feeling of All Goodness. Maybe it only lasted for a second but in that second all things felt so good.

Maybe you were doing something that motivated it. Maybe it was someone who caused you to feel it. Maybe it just happened. However it occurred, remember that feeling.

As we get older in life, these feelings of overall expansive goodness seemingly do not appear as frequently. There is any number of psychological reasons for this, but does that have to be the case? Or, is it simply you not allowing yourself to be free enough to embrace the perfection of your reality?

So here, try this experiment. Just STOP right now. Close your eyes and let go of the all and the everything that you are thinking and feeling that is making you feel all of the non-perfect things you may be perceiving. Just let it all go.

Now, find that place in you that is the essence of feeling good and whole-life connected. It's in there. Maybe you have not allowed yourself to feel it for a long time but it is there. Look for it. Touch it. Feel it. Don't make excuses why you can't feel it, just let it overtake you.

Here's the thing about life, as you grow older, more and more things become expected. More and more things become known. As you know them, they are not new—they are not experiential. But, it doesn't have to be that way. Next time you are doing anything, experiencing that anything as if it is the first time you have ever done it. With this, everything becomes new. Everything feels fresh. Everything can be your pathway to the Peak Experience.

Let go, be free, allow yourself to encounter the Peak Experience.

Zen Filmmaking Sidebar
16/Jan/2022 03:07 PM

  I want to write a quick little sidebar here for all of you *Zen Filmmaking* aficionados out there as I have recently been receiving a lot of questions about some of the very obscure Zen Film titles. In some cases, after I have answered, some people haven't believed me and have pointed me to places on the inter-web where people are proclaiming supposed storylines about these films with some even claiming that they have viewed them or that they are hidden somewhere in the realm of cinema never-never-land only to be uncovered by the dedicated cinema sleuth. Wrong!

  In the 1990s, Don Jackson had a high-end print design company under contract. Due to this fact, some of the films that either he, Mark Williams, or myself had come up with, (and we were planning to shoot), had posters designed for them. In some cases, even press kits for these upcoming projects were put together. As Julie Strain was an integral part of the team back then, some of these posters and theater cards featured an image of her. Because they were so well designed, she presented these posters in some of her books and her playing card sets published by her then husband, Kevin Eastman, under his *Heavy Metal* publication label. The thing to know is, however, these films were never made. Yes, there are films like *Lingerie Kickboxer* that were filmed and edited but probably will never see the light of day for various reasons. And, films like *The Strain Sister's Shockumentary* and *Vampire Child* that were filmed but never edited and the footage will never be shown. But, all the rest of those titles, they do not exist!

  On another side of this issue, it is very common in the world of filmmaking that some films are retitled. Thus, the same movie may have more than one or even multiple titles. This is the case with a number of the films created by Donald G. Jackson and myself. Same movie, different title.

In some cases, people have come to believe that these are two different films and if they can just get their hands on a copy of the movie, with that other title, it will prove to be a different film. Again, this is an incorrect thought process. And, though you may see people making this claim or that claim about a film on-line, no matter what they are saying that does not make it the truth. The film they are talking about was simply retitled for marketing purposes.

I suppose that I could provide a list of the films here that some people have read or have heard about or have even claimed to have viewed but I'm sure I would forget one or more of them. So, I will just state it, again, they do not exist!

If you're looking for information about a Zen Film and if you can't find that information here, on this website, or via the formal sites that focus on the films of established filmmakers then that Scott Shaw or Donald G. Jackson film, someone is talking about, is not a film that was actually produced. Don't be deceived by the comments and the claims people make about these non-existent films.

I am in possession of master copies of all of the films created by Donald G. Jackson and myself. As well as I have all of the original footage. It is all locked up tight in my temperature controlled film vault over at the studio. If I don't know about a Zen Film, and if I don't own a copy of it, I can categorically tell you, it was never created. So, don't waste your time trying to find it.

In closing, I hope this sidebar provides you with a bit more of an unencumbered Life Time as you now know you don't have to try to find a film that was never produced. Of course, if you have any other questions or want to get in touch with me about something the best way to do it is via Facebook.

Be positive and smile. And, don't believe everything you hear or read on the internet. Thanks for all the love!

Where Did You Get Your Misinformation?
16/Jan/2022 09:00 AM

You'll have to excuse me, but I am continually brought back to the question of where did someone get the information that they are so bolding proclaiming when what they are purporting is completely wrong?

I think we've all seen it. Maybe some of you do it. But, motivated by whatever, some people hope to tell the story of life and art and god and history and people, and science to others but what happens when what they are saying is wrong? Do they care that they are wrong? No. Do they change their words, apologize for their mistakes, when they are told they are wrong? No. They just keep proclaiming their lie. How about you?

Though there has forever been a means for someone or something to emphatically proclaim what they believe; be it truthful or not, since the dawning of the internet all of this has become so much easier. Just by believing it, just by saying it, a lie has the potential to become the understood and the accepted truth.

In the age of the internet, somebody decides something is true. Maybe they go and proclaim it on some website or on a site like Wikipedia where anyone can pretty much say anything and there it becomes the accepted truth; even though it may not be truthful at all. Yet, people make their proclamations and as wrong as they may be they find their believers. But, what is belief if you believe a lie?

There is so much misinformation out there is in really brain numbing.

I get it, most people hear what they hear and immediately believe it as long as it is presented in a formidable manner. But, that does not necessarily make it the truth.

Then, there are those who are such contrarians that they will proclaim even the purest of proven truths are false.

So, what are we left with? Answer: a world based on false beliefs originated in lies.

I can say to you: seek only the truth, believe only the truth, and speak only the truth. But, how many people across the world even care enough about spending the time to find that truth that they will actually do it? They just want to believe what they hear. It's easy. How about you?

Some may argue that truth is an individual perspective. But, is it? Is the truth simply based in what you believe or is it based in some greater something? And, if you believe a lie, if you speak a lie, does that lie ever become the truth?

So much of life is opened to interpretation. So much of a lie is defined by belief. But, what is interpretation and what is belief? Are either of those the truth? No. They are just individualized mind stuff.

Who are you, what are you, and what do you wish to base your life upon? Where have you gained your knowledge? Moreover, what gives you the right to speak your knowledge when, at best, your knowledge was and is only the interpretation of someone else's truth?

You may not care about any of this. You may only wish to believe whatever it is you decide to believe, provided to you by whomever. You may even wish to go and speak the knowledge you believe you possess to the world. But, if all of your knowledge is based upon nothing more than someone else's lie or someone else's misinterpretation of someone else's searched for truth than all you have become is a liar or a believer in a lie. How does that make you feel?

Take the time to find the truth or all of your beliefs become nothing more than a lie.

* * *
16/Jan/2022 07:17 AM

If you're not offered an option, then you have no choice to make.

Rollergator
15/Jan/2022 02:00 PM

Since the Rifftrax version of *Rollergator* hit YouTube, I've been receiving a lot of questions about the film. To briefly answer some of these questions and to clear up some misunderstandings about the film, for those of you who care, I put up a page about the film. You can check it out here: *Rollergator*.

Here is the piece I wrote about *Rollergator* that appears on that page. I hope you will find it interesting. Though, of course, there is a lot more things I could say about that film, I trust this will provide you with a clearer perspective about this movie. If I am asked some very specific questions that deserve to be answered or if I come up with some additional thoughts on the film I will probably add that supplementary information to that page. Enjoy…

Rollergator

Rollergator is a film originally conceived by Donald G. Jackson and Scott Shaw.

The evolution of Rollergator began shortly after Donald G. Jackson was fired from directing the film, *Pocket Ninjas*. Donald G. Jackson conceived Pocket Ninjas as a young adult tribute to the Zen Film, *The Roller Blade Seven*. When he was hired to direct this film he had Mark Williams compose the screenplay for this movie. Though Jackson was serious in his planned attempt to recreate the cinematic imagery of *The Roller Blade Seven* and pay tribute to the film, he also possessed a hidden agenda as he did with all of his filmmaking endeavors. He cast certain people in this film who he wanted to exasperate and diminish. Thus, the adult leads of this film were treated to a style of filmmaking and an attitude of a director that they had never encountered. Eventually, Jackson was let go as director of *Pocket Ninjas* as the producer saw the film as never being completed in a marketable manner if he allowed Jackson to continue forward with his haphazard style of filmmaking.

PS: And, this is a piece just for this blog: Though I am credited as being an actor in the film, *Pocket Ninjas,* I did not actually perform in that movie. My scene in that film was an unused scene, taken from another film, I had done with the producer. To continue…

Very soon after this, Jackson was courted by a film financing company that wished to capitalize on Jackson's success with such films as, *Hell Comes to Frogtown.* From this, and as a believed means of retribution to the producer of *Pocket Ninjas* for his being relieved from his director duties on the movie, Jackson set about making three cult film orientated movies, seemingly geared towards the younger audience. The first of which was, *Rollergator.* This film was also loosely inspired by *The Roller Blade Seven.* The other two films were: *Little Lost Sea Serpent* and *Baby Ghost.* Though there were and maybe still are some people who claim these movies to be children's films, for anyone who watches these movies they will clearly see the hidden, very adult orientated themes.

The concept for *Rollergator* was conceived by Donald G. Jackson and Scott Shaw. The screenplay for *Rollergator* was written by Mark Williams. Thus, *Rollergator* is not a Zen Film like many people believe is the case. It is a script-based cinematic experiment.

The reason Donald G. Jackson commonly based his films upon screenplays is that he wanted the framework of a proposed completed production to present to his investors, his cast, and his crew. This is in stark contrast to the films he created with Scott Shaw at the helm, where no screenplays were ever employed. Though, in truth, many viewers fail to see a more concrete storyline being presented in these script-based movies.

The production of this film took place in the style of pure guerrilla filmmaking. There were no filming permits or stagnant set locations. This movie was filmed in many of the locations commonly see in the films of Donald G. Jackson, located around the Southern California area.

As the female lead of this film was under the age of eighteen at the time of its production, her mother was constantly on the set when her character was being filmed. This kept the crazed reactionary behavior of Donald G. Jackson in check during, at least, those stages of this production.

It is stated on several places on the internet, and even on the Internet Movie Database, that Donald G. Jackson did the voice of Baby Gator in *Rollergator*. This is not the case, however. The voice in both *Rollergator,* and where Conrad Brooks revises his *Rollergator* role in *Max Hell Frog Warrior,* was performed by a production assistant who worked for Jackson during that period of time.

In has often been questioned, does the *Rollergator* still exist? The answer to that question is, no. At one point, Jackson when into one of his rages in the office, and he pulled *Rollergator* apart. Thus, it is no more.

Since its completion, *Rollergator* has come to be embraced by a very wide audience. It was distributed to many countries across the globe where it initially found a home in the then thriving video tape market. Today, it remains at the centerpoint of cult film criticism; receiving both praise and scorn.

In 2015, the creative team at Rifftrax licensed this film and have created one of their amusing verbal parodies of the movie, thereby cementing Rollergator into the archives of the cult film elite. Many more thousands of people have viewed this movie via the Rifftrax version than those that have seen the original rendition of the film.

Further Blog Only Information: *Rollergator* was uploaded to YouTube in 2021. Due to the contract Rifftrax has with YouTube, if you search for Rollergator on YouTube the official and full-length version of the film will not come up, however. All that you will see in the search is reviews of the film. If you want to take a look a *Rollergator* on YouTube click on the title.

* * *
14/Jan/2022 12:21 PM

The moment you feel you are better and more than someone or that they are less you have lost the key to your humanity.

* * *
14/Jan/2022 07:21 AM

Just because you claim you don't remember doing something does not mean you didn't do it.

157

You're Not That Spiritual
13/Jan/2022 04:20 PM

Depending on what circles you hang out in, you are going to run into a lot of people claiming a lot of spirituality. *"I am. You are not."* But, have you ever noticed that the people who claim spiritually are the most misdirected, biased, judgmental people you will ever meet? If I can step out on a limb here, they are some of the most hypocritical people you will ever encounter. It always seems that they have a reason or a justification for doing and saying what they do or say but the moment anyone else does something they don't like that person is immediately condemned.

Most people don't really care about spirituality. Yes, they may call themselves a whatever. They may claim to follow this religion or that. But, that is not the essence of their life or their brand. There are other people, however, who make all kinds of proclamations and even make their living via embracing one or more of the various realms of spirituality. The problem is, most of these people are so self-focused that they demean and attempt to hurt the life of anyone who believes or follows a different path than they do. Is that true spirituality?

Even me, I have been attacked because I too write about spirituality and/or its various classifications. Some people, believing whatever it is they believe, maybe read one of my books or something and they deduce I am a some kind of a something. Then, when they see one of my films or maybe a photograph I took or read one of my provocative poems they come at me as being fake or unholy or something like that. They unfollow me on Instagram or unfriend me on Facebook. *"Goodbye. Who cares!"* Some even write to me telling me about how what they think I am doing is wrong and/or how what I am doing is not spiritual. Really???

Here's the thing, and this goes for all of those people who cast their judgements onto others, not just via the realms of spiritually, you can never truly know who or what a person is inside. This is especially true of you do not personally know that individual. At best, all you can do is judge someone based upon your own predetermined biases. But, if you do that, what does that say about you? How does that describe the person you truly are? Are you so all-powerfully spiritual that you can see into the soul of another individual and know why they do what they do? Can you psychically peer into their past and view any life traumas that caused them to emerge as the person they have became? Or, are you simply someone so locked into the physical plane of existence that all you see is what you believe to be the obvious? How spiritual is that?

For anyone who truly understands spirituality, they understand that there are so many levels to spiritually, defined by so many different traditions and understandings, that there is never only one definition of spirituality. Are the Tantric Yogis sinner because they embrace sex in their meditative practices. Are the Indigenous-Americans or the Siddhi Yogis of India sinners because they partake of hallucinogenics? It's all just a point of view.

Yes, you may like or not like, understand or not understand, believe or disbelieve what another person practices as their road to spiritual understanding, but just because you don't like it or do not believe in it that does not make it wrong.

This is an important thing to keep in mind as your pass through your life. It is an important point to take to heart as you look at the life of other people. It is especially an essential point to keep in mind if you are someone who is consciously walking on the spiritual path.

If someone judges you, know that they are lost into the mindset of self-righteous indignation based upon ego not truth. If you find yourself judging others, catch yourself and stop it!

If you wish to embrace true spirituality you must allow everyone to walk their own path. If they are right and righteous, their life will prove it out. If they are wrong and unholy, their karma will catch up with them. But remember, no one: not you, not me, or anyone has the right to judge another person about spirituality or anything else. As we are not that other person, we can never truly understand what makes them do what they do, believe what they believe, or what causes them to act out their role on this life stage in the manner that they portray.

The Audition Process
12/Jan/2022 10:33 AM

  For anyone who has ever stepped into the film industry and desired to be an actor they understand that the audition process is one of the cornerstones of making your way onto the silver screen. But, the fact of the matter is, the audition process is completely misunderstood or perhaps better put not understood and, in fact, it is more of a place of power-tripping and dominance than of finding the right person for a role.
  Let me explain… Though there are certainly methods for new actors and actresses to find their way to an audition via means like self-submitting to projects that they find on-line. Just like, back in the day, there were weekly newspapers devoted to the independent industry that came out where filmmakers, myself included, would post casting notices. But, many of the projects, at that level, were and are fake. But, I'll get to that in a moment.
  This being said, the dream of all actors is to get an agent. But, how do agents make their money? Sure, they get ten percent of all that their clients makes when they are acting in a verified production. But, if you look to the client list of most agents, their clients are not working. Then what?
  For you actors out there, have you ever wondered why when you get a new agent, they demand you get new headshot from a photographer they recommend? Answer, they get a kick back. Do you ever question why they want you to take acting classes at a specific acting school? Kick back.
  After this, the process gets even more convoluted. What an agent does is to try to get his or her clients an audition. How do they do this? By submitting their actor's headshots to the casting director of a project and maybe even giving them a call. If their client does get an audition, again there is a secret exchange of money. A small fee is paid. That

is why agents get so upset with their clients if they blow off an audition. They make no money. It is all an intermingled spider web that most people, even those actors in the game, never come to understand.

Post this point, the audition process becomes even more tangled…

As I have long warned any new actor or actress in the industry, and you can read this in many of my writings on the subject, if the project you are auditioning for is not a union project you need to be very-very careful. First of all, there are many would-be filmmakers out there who hope to make a movie, and maybe even believe that they can and will make that film, but so many of these independent projects fall apart. It's just the nature of the beast.

In some cases, people who are claiming to make a film are simply looking for girlfriends, boyfriends, or just hook-ups and they use the audition process to do just that. So again, you need to be very-very careful.

Even in the A-market, as we have all now heard, there are some extremely bad deeds done by filmmakers to actors and actresses. Some of these people, like Harvey Weinstein, were behind some truly great films. Yet, they have turned out to be predatory monsters. Though people like Weinstein were at the top, the list goes on and on and downwards from there. There are the actors who hope to be in films and there are the predatory people who use that desire to meet their own whims. How do those predators meet their prey? Auditions.

But, it is really more than that. The audition process is a labyrinth of power-tripping and deceitful actions that most people, even those in the middle of the game, do not understand.

I can tell you about a couple of my own experiences that you may find amusing. Early in my acting career, I went to an audition over on the Warner Bothers lot. Whenever an actor, including myself, got an audition on one of the major film lots it was and is a big deal. Anyway, I do the audition and that was that. I didn't know what film is was for. Maybe a year or so later I'm at the movie *Speed* with one of my friends and there is was, the scene I had auditioned for. I couldn't believe it. Why would they audition a nobody like me for a role that was obviously going to a star name? They would never have given me that role, though, of course, I wish they would have. Why did they do that? Answer: It's just part of the game. In many cases they audition people just to make it look like they are doing their job. It pumps the dreams of the actor up but it equals very little. Again, another sad truth of the audition process.

  In another case, around this same period of time, I auditioned for a commercial. I was called by my agent, a little bit down the road, and I had apparently booked it. Great! I was very happy. I go to the set and the first thing this very-very gay director, (and I'm not throwing shots here, I am just describing the situation), comes up and puts his hands on my face, pulls me close to him, looks me over and demeaningly says, *"I've got someone so much better than you."* What!

  Anyway… This other actor was apparently late or indecisive about being there or something? Maybe an hour later, after I've gone through makeup and everything, the guy walks through the door. Good looking guy and all but nothing special. The director runs up and kisses him on the lips. The 1st AD comes over and send me home. Okay… I guess I was the second choice.

  Now, this was a union gig. What they did was totally against union policies. If they bring you on a set, even if they don't use you, they have to pay you. Me, I got nothing except a little upset. I told my agent what happened, she did nothing. I guess I could have filed a complaint with SAG but I had already learned they don't stand behind their actors so what would be the point? Thus, what did that audition equal? Nothing but a big waste of my time. And remember, I'm not the only one. This kind of stuff goes on all the time. Again, the truth of the audition process...

As a filmmaker, I used to do the audition process. ...At least sometimes. It depended on who I was working with. But, I never really like it. I always preferred just the meet-and-greet. I mean, you can get a pretty good understanding of who and what a person is by just meeting them. But, even via this process, I have sometimes been very disappointed by the attitude an actor brought to the set. But, as I am speaking about auditioning here, I won't go into that. And besides, you know me, I'm all about the Zen. I always do things a little differently...

Since we have entered into this era of #metoo, a lot of actresses and/or actors have stepped up and spoken out about some bad behavior delivered to them by some very noted filmmakers. Some of the complains about what took place and what was expected occurred during the audition process. I won't list those situations here as you can find them on-line and I am sure it is more revealing to have the story told via the words of the victims. But, think about it, if that took place and still takes place on the A-level, think about what is going on within the indie level where there is no implied guarantee of protection. I think a lot of people have been hurt. Who helped those people who were hurt? Not the production companies and not the unions.

Long ago, as an actor, I stopped going to auditions. It was such a game of bullshit and hope building equaling very little. I've spoken about this in the past, but you get all dressed-up in-character, drive across the city to get there on time, check in and wait. Then, they call you in, you read your lines, you give your best performance, then drive home through traffic. A total day killer. After that, maybe you get a call-back. I seemed to get those a lot. Then, you go through the whole process again. Maybe there is a third or a fourth call-back if it is for a film. But then, nothing... In many cases the commercial was never filmed or the movie was never made. Or, they cast someone else… What did all that time, all that auditioning equal? Nothing.

I feel I have been more than lucky in the roles I have received via auditions. But, compare that to the hundreds of auditions I went on and the ratio is very small. Now, think about the thousands-upon-thousands of actors and actresses who have gone through this same process. Thus, long ago, I stopped. I mean, many of the roles I received I did not have to audition for. And, if you want me as an actor, and your project is real, call me up or call my manager. We can have a sit down but I ain't gonna audition. You either know what I'm about by this stage of my career or not.

But, that's just me. Everyone isn't like that. Most actors are not filmmakers. I know people that have been going to audition for decades. Some even used to have TV shows or acted in big films. Now, today, they are just trying to get another dose of the dream. Thus, they go head-to-head with all of the new faces on the scene of which there is a constantly changing array.

The thing is and the point being, hoping to get into the film game via going to auditions is like being thrown into the gladiator pit. You have to be a trained fighter or you are going to get creamed. You have to know what to expect, and kept your expectation low, or you will walk away very hurt. The thing is, most people come to Hollywood with stars in their eyes. But, just because you get a headshot, just because you go to acting class, just because you get an agent, just because you go to an audition, does not mean that you are going to get the role in that big film which will lead you to stardom.

In closing, be careful, because it is a dark game. People only care about themselves. And, if you do go to an audition, keep your guard up, because you do not know who is going to be the auditionor. Even if they have a big name in industry, that does not mean that they will not try to do bad things.

When I'm Dead
12/Jan/2022 07:58 AM

Do you ever think about what you want to happen to your body when you die? For most, they are so lost into living that they never think about that kind of thing. That's good. Why should they?

I know my parents planned for the future. ...Their future demise. They bought their gravesites at a cemetery in Inglewood and all that. My father was planted there—long before I imagine he anticipated that moment would occur. My mother never made it that far, however. She died near one of my distant cousins in the AZ and I wasn't informed until far after the fact. What happened to her body, I will never know? The woman, my distant cousin, was, (how can I say this nicely), far from truthful. My mother had another family gravesite waiting for her back in her hometown in the Midwest, in amongst all of her close relatives, as well. Also empty and unused.

I guess it's a good thing, planning for your demise. My father and other relatives had their gravesites and their funeral expenses all paid for before they died. When my mother-in-law passed away last year from COVID-19 it was a big surprise that she had an insurance policy that covered all the expenses. Good gesture, I think. It saves the grieving from worrying about all that—the who's going to pay for what, etc...

Near the end of my *Zen Filmmaking* brother, Donald G. Jackson's life, (as he was one of those people who was warned by the doctors that the end was approaching fast), he got all obsessed with visiting the graves of those people he admired. He would drag me to cemeteries all the time searching for the gravesites of this person or that. Weird...

I hear people like to go and fuck on the grave of Jim Morrison in Paris. I've spent a lot of time in Paris but I've never gone to his gravesite. I'm all about living as long as you can live. I love living. I love the living. Then, once a person has moved on they have moved on. Let them go. Though what they have created may live on for eternity, the dead are dead. Why go and visit their grave?

    I don't have a gravesite waiting for me or anything like that. Though I suppose I could lay claim to the two awaiting my mother. But, that's just not me. No funeral. No open casket ceremony. No preacher speaking what preachers do at a funeral. No teary-eyed gatherings. No mourners shoveling the dirt, one-by-one, on top of my way too expensive coffin that no-one will ever see again. No sticking flowers into the little hole thing at the base of every tombstone. I'll just be cremated and tossed into the ocean. That way, if you ever want to come and visit me or if you want to fuck on my grave all you have to do is dive into the divine mother ocean. There I will be. Then, but not now… I still have way too much life to live.

* * *
11/Jan/2022 12:12 PM

If all you have is what you had, then you have nothing.

*   *   *

11/Jan/2022 12:02 PM

Once you realize you've missed your train there's no more reason to rush to get to the train station.

* * *

11/Jan/2022 09:31 AM

What did you do to correct the last mistake that you made?

* * *
11/Jan/2022 09:23 AM

What's important to you today probably won't be what's important to you tomorrow. Remember that as you make your life choices.

Doing Verse Undoing
11/Jan/2022 07:59 AM

As we have just entered into a new year, it is a time when some people attempt to make a change. They make, *"New Year's Resolutions,"* and things like that. Though I've never been one to employee the New Year's Resolution tool, I do see its benefits. There it is, a day when all things become new. But, the fact of the matter is, every day is a new day where all things become new. Any day can be your, *"New Day."*

Whenever people make New Year's Resolutions and/or decide to make a change, it always seems that it is about the doing. It never seems to be about the undoing. People want to lose weight, they want to get out of financial debt, the want to get out of that bad relationship, they want to get a new job or a new car. Of course, the list goes on and on. But, whatever it is they are thinking about doing, it is based in the, *"Wanting,"* which equals the, *"Doing."*

Think about your own life. What do you wish were different? Did you make a New Year's Resolution to make it different? Do you ever/have you ever set about on a course to make that change?

The thing is, when people set a goal those goals require, *"Doing."* But, so few people possess the ability to actually, *"Do."* They may think they want to, *"Do."* They may believe that they can, *"Do."* But, doing takes focused effort which is something very few people possess. They may do it for a day or a week but then their doing gets the best of them, and it is just another New Year's Resolution left undone.

On a deeper investigation of this issue, do you ever think about your doing? Isn't your doing all done for you? How many New Year's Resolutions have you made where your doing is completely focused on doing for someone or something else? And, did you/do you ever ponder this? The thing is, *"Doing,"* is most commonly, *"Done,"* for yourself. Is that how your life should operate?

From the perspective of Zen, *"Doing,"* is the exact opposite of what a person should actually be doing. Instead they should be, *"Undoing."* How must time do you spend undoing? Aside from the occasional Spring Cleaning, how much emptying and purifying do you do? How much time do you spend doing to stop the Have? How much time do you spend removing?

There are so many levels of life that people could live from a better and more pure perspective but due to their focus on themselves they do not. They only think about themselves and their gain. If their gain hurts someone or something else, so be it. Do they/do you spend any time undoing the damage onto who or what you have hurt while you were doing what you do, equaling getting what you want?

If your doing hurts, then should that doing be done? If your doing hurts, and you have not undone that hurtful doing, doesn't that hurtful doing come to be the definition of your life? Most people never even ponder this fact. Most people never attempt to undo their hurtful doing. Not them who is hurt, why should they care?

Very few people ever care to undo the doing that they have done in this physical world. Why? Because they are a selfish creature. And, this is where all of the bad deeds in the doings are done.

From a perspective of consciousness, how much time do you guide your mind to mental undoing? For most, they spend all of their waking hours thinking about whatever it is on their mind. They never stop the, *"Do."* But, from this, no new and/or better levels of consciousness can ever be experienced. I get it, most people don't care. But, they should. Because, ask yourself, *"How truly happy are you?" "How spiritually aware are you?" "How pure are your actions leading to the dos that they do?" "How does your doing affect you and, more importantly, how does your doing affect others?"* Moreover, *"What is the ultimate price you will pay for what you have, are, and will do?"*

Doing is a natural state of life. But, it does not have to be your only state of life. You can be more than simply guided by the doing to get what you want. You can be more than what your doing does to others. You can be more than simply a mindless individual walking the path of their life guided by nothing more than Doing to Get.

In doing there is never undoing. But, your life doesn't have to be that way. Try the undoing. Experience the silence. Do that and an entirely new, cleaner, purer, and better reality will be opened up for you.

Do the undo.

* * *
11/Jan/2022 07:58 AM

If you don't accept who you used to be you can never become anything new.

* * *
11/Jan/2022 07:57 AM

Every day that you don't do it another day goes by and it is not done.

The Critic's Mind
10/Jan/2022 07:56 AM

  There is the saying, *"You can't help anyone until you can help yourself."* The problem and I guess the good thing about statements like this is that they are open to individual interpretation. When I hear this statement I have been lead to believe it means that a person must first become a better person: they must be taught, they must study, they must learn, they must focus on their personal evolution via physical, educational, psychological, and spiritual means and then by having elevated themselves to a new and better projection of the Self they may then extend their hand to help others. But, how many people in life ever try to do any of that? They hear, *"Help yourself,"* and they focus only on the Self: the Lower Self, never the Higher Self.
  If you look around at life, maybe even look at your own life, people fill their time with distraction. Whether that distraction is shopping, taking art or acting classes, going to the gym, or a bar, people look for a way to make their life seem like something more. They do this, but they never seem to focus on the things that could actually make them a better person.
  Even look to sports. Think how many people become all consumed by watching sports.
  Very few people ever raise their bodies to the level of being able to participate in sports on the professional level. This is primarily because of the fact that very few people possess the dedication to train their body to the degree that they could perform at that level. Yet, look around and listen to the world, there are millions and millions of fans across the globe who wish to put out their critique and their criticism about what is taking place on that field, on that court, or in that ring.
  This takes us to the point of all of this. Criticism is easy. It takes very little effort. But, it is no more than a life

based upon the drug of distraction because it take no true training or achievement to become a critic. Yet, do the critics realize that what they are doing serves no beneficial purpose to the greater good of humanity or to themselves? The answer to this question is obviously, no.

I think to the world of film, literature, and music where I am involved. In particular, at least for this piece, I will focus on the world of film. I look to earlier times. Then, it was the small magazines that were stocked full of film critiques. Magazines like *Draculina, Psychotronic, Shock Cinema, Oriental Cinema, Independent Cinema, B-Movie Magazine* and others focused on the No to Low Budget arena of filmmaking. The thing that always struck me was that most of these magazines, (but not all), were operated by people who had never made a film. The reviews were written by critics who had never been on a set or understood what it took to actually envision, produce, edit, and then distribute a film; especially on the independent level. Yet, they wrote their reviews about other people's films and presented them to the world.

Though times have changed and, for the most part, this level of film reviewing has moved to the internet, the problem has remained the same. The people doing the reviewing are not true filmmakers. They are not people who hold the passion for filmmaking and will do whatever it takes to get their film completed. They simple want to take the easy way out: maybe sit in front of a camera, maybe grab some clips from some other filmmaker's film, and talk about it.

The thing that has always surprised me the most about this process, especially at the independent film level, is that these reviewers at least claim to have a love for the craft. By focusing on this level of filmmaking they are proclaiming that they like this stratum of filmmaking. Yet, they tear these films apart. Films that are made on a minuscule budget. Films that, at best, must be seen for what they are. Yet, these critics isolate and attempt to interpreter, via their own prejudice, and go after the smallest item(s) they believe to be a flaw, attempting to make themselves appear to be some grand interpreter by spouting out their beliefs. But, how does that make anything better? How does that make the world better? How does that make the listener better? And, most importantly, how does that make the critic a more enlightened or refined individual? How does that even make them a what they are critiquing; namely a filmmaker?

I am using those people that talk about that something Out-There as an example. I do this because if you think about it, ponder how many people live their life based on this premise. They speak about this, they speak about that, they find that drug of distraction via that thing Out-There that has very little to do with the overall greater evolution of their life or the World Mind.

Why do so many people do this? Because it is easy. Because it is a drug. Because it allows them to not have to focus on themselves. By placing the focus outside of themselves, they do not have to look within. They do not have to calculate their own flaws and faults. They do not have to become that better person they could be if they only tired.

Think about your own life, what are you doing to make yourself that better person? I am not talking about what are you doing to be more powerful, be more loved by the masses of people you will never know, I am not speaking about you getting that better car or that bigger TV, what I am asking is, what are you doing to bring your body and your mind into a higher state of being where you would actually possess the ability to truly help other people or the world as a whole? If you don't have an answer for this, that is your answer. Maybe you should reevaluate your life. *"You can't help anyone until you can help yourself."*

The Questions You Can Never Ask
09/Jan/2022 08:27 AM

Last week, the great film director Peter Bogdanovich passed away. He was one of those seminal directors that somehow fell from grace in the film industry long before he should have. He did some great-great films early in his career and some exceptional little-known works past that point. Why he fell from grace, I do not know? But, nonetheless, he did.

I never met Bogdanovich. I guess that is my fault as I never tried. Growing up in Hollywood, I was just never that impressed with celebrity. That has always caused me to kind of avoid the whole, *"Industry,"* thAng. This being said, Bogdanovich was one of those filmmakers that I wish I could have asked several questions about the hows and the whys. But, now he is gone. I can't ask.

Back in the day, Don Jackson was on top of the all and the everything Hollywood. Hailing from the Midwest, he was far more Star Stuck than I could ever be. He was really on top of things and he got us invited to a lot of the very high-end industry gatherings where we would rub elbows with the Hollywood elite. Again, at the time, I was never that impressed. But, looking back, I can say that those were some very interesting and memorable events. The stories I could tell… Though there were tons of connections I probably should have made and questions I should have ask, I simply existed in my own Zen.

As you may know, my father died when I was ten. I was just a kid. The thing about being a kid is that you do not ask a person a lot of those probing questions that you do as you get older. You don't find out those life defining factors that lead them to be who and what they became. As he died when I was so young, I never questioned some of the questions that have remained in my mind. At best, I got second-hand answers. But, can second-hand answers ever truly be believed? Thus, there are many things about my father that I will never know.

When I look out to the world, I see and hear that a lot of people know a lot of things about a lot of people. They make all of these claims about someone based upon what??? Speculation at best because they never asked that person about their truth. What kind of knowledge is that? The fact is, it is not knowledge at all, it is simply ego-inspired guess work.

The point of all of this is, you really need to ask questions. You really need to ask questions of and from the people you have questions for. Because if you don't, they will die and you will never know the truth of a true answer.

* * *
09/Jan/2022 07:51 AM

You can't go somewhere that no longer exists.

* * *
08/Jan/2022 07:28 AM

How many people are asking God for help right now?

Next time you ask God for help consider who else is asking for help at that moment and why?

Then consider, do you deserve God's help?

* * *
07/Jan/2022 04:55 PM

The minute you think you're right and someone else is wrong all of the problems of the world begin.

The Big Lie
07/Jan/2022 09:57 AM

It's kind of funny... Someone friended me on Facebook and as soon as I accepted they sent me this message, *"Greetings would you like to join the Illuminati so you can be rich, famous, and wealthy and have a total life change forever. This is the first time in history, our organization is seeking for new member. Do you accept becoming a member."* I guess they don't know that I already am a member of the Illuminati.

So, here's the story... For those of you who have cared enough to know anything about me, you may already know, but one of the paths I have chosen to follow was that I have passed from beginning to end within the Rosicrucian Order. I'm fully initiated all they way through. I can use F.R.C. after my name but I have never been one of those people into titles.

Though my tendencies have always leaned towards Eastern Metaphysics, I always felt that if you want to truly understand any tradition you really need to delve deeply and whole heartedly into that tradition. That's what I did. I joined and fully passed through the various levels associated with the Rosicrucian and the Martinist Order.

Somewhere along the way, after being fully initiated, I received a document telling me that due to my devotion, (or whatever term they used), that I was now a member of the Illuminati. I guess some people would fall all over themselves if they got a letter like that. Me, it just kind of amused me. I have all that stuff somewhere. I'm not quite sure where it is or I would have quoted it to you exactly. But, looking for it is just too much of a problem, at least for the goings-on of the right now.

Illuminati, there is always this grand illusion associated with what that means and who is associated with such an all-powerful mystical group in control of the world.

I mean, the rich and the powerful have always controlled the world. Nothing new there. But, there is that illusion that if you could join that group, everything about your everything would become better.

Last night, I watched one of the documentaries about QAnon. It talked about their belief that an all-powerful qabalah of Left Wing cannibalistic pedophiles have worked against the betterment of the Right Wing and all life in general. I won't go into a long definition about QAnon here as I'm sure anything I may say someone would find fault in. So, if you want to know more, just look it up, information is all over the place.

Though I have studied deeply into this subject, watched several of the docs, and find the origins and the presentation of their all and their everything very-very interesting, hand-in-hand with this, yesterday was January 6th, the one year anniversary of the U.S. insurrection. From this, all I kept hearing on the TV and the radio were people referring to, *"The Big Lie."* For those of you who may not know, what this refers to is the fact that many people believe that the last presidential election was stolen from Trump but the liberal media all call it, *"The Big Lie."* Meaning, the people who believe this are wrong—they believe a lie.

I could not help but think what a great marketing tool that term is. That's what marketing is, bringing an idea down to its most elemental level so you can sell it to the public. Now, whether you believe the election was stolen or not, is not even important, at least not important in regard to this marketing ploy. What somebody did was to come up with a great catch phrase that people can use to make the other side look stupid if they believe what they believe. Not right. But, think about it, how much of this style of marketing takes place all the time? Someone thinks of some way to attack the bliss of someone else and then they put it into a phrase that can be easily disseminated.

...Whether it is true or not does not even matter. They have a tool to separate the people.

Here in the U.S., the TV talking heads are constantly speaking about how divided the U.S. currently is. ...That it is the most divided it has ever been throughout history. I don't believe that. For example, think about the 1960s when the Vietnam War was raging and young Americans were dying for no reason—including one of my close family-members. Then, there was big division. There were protests all the time. Combine that with the fact that during this same period of time there was a racial and cultural revolution taking place. Then, the county was truly a divided mess.

But, then as now, the people who are talking about the division are the ones who are creating the division. Last night, the President of the United States in a speech attacked and insulted the former President. How wrong is that? The President of the United States of American should be more discerning than that. They should present a more refined image of themselves and the country to the world. Whether you love or hate the current or the former president, verbally attacking someone never makes anything any better. It just causes further anger and separation. How does that help? Moreover, how does claiming to believe in one thing while insultingly diminishing the beliefs of someone else make anything any better for anyone?

"The Big Lie," is that the people who are using that terminology are creating the division—they are making things worse, they are making nothing any better.

But, as in all things life, there are always those people at the top of the food chain pulling the strings. Maybe they are the rich, maybe they are the powerful, maybe they are the cannibalistic pedophiles referenced by QAnon, maybe they are the Illuminati. Whoever they are, whomever they employ to come up with great catch phrases like, *"The Big Lie,"* all they do is to divide an already divided world. They create and worship the, *"Haves,"* while they diminish the everyone else. Power, Prestige, Wealth, and False Fame, you can keep it. I'd rather meet the world with a smile and try to make everyone's everything just a little bit better with the small amount of help that I may be able to provide. Join the Illuminati; thanks but no thanks.

On the Basis of Arrogance
06/Jan/2022 12:16 PM

I believe if we look around ourselves we can view arrogance and self-entitlement all the time. This is not the say that most people follow this pattern of behavior but, this being the case, you don't have to look too far until you will encounter it.

There are the very blatant forms of arrogance. Those people who just project and perhaps even tell you that they are better than you. Then, there is the more sublet forms of arrogance: people using titles in front of their name, people boasting, people telling others how much they known compared to how little other people know, people who let you know that they are rich and you are not so, *"Look out,"* people who are big or muscular or tough looking and let you know that they can easily kick your ass, and the list goes on.

Anyway, what brought me to all of this was today a curious incident occurred. I was driving to the post office. I was in the left turn lane, my arrow came on, and I began to make my turn. This guy, waiting for the light to turn his direction, just lays into his horn on me. First, I thought maybe he didn't realize he had a red light or something like that but that was not the case as his car didn't move. He just sat there honking at me with a scowl on his face and wording something??? Why? I have no idea.

The guy was probably in his eighties. He was driving a newish convertible Aston Martin. My first though was, *"You're a bit old to be having a midlife crisis,"* but, whatever… I just let those acts of arrogance go. Why allow them to control my life-space?

I drive a bit farther and as I am attempting to turn into the post office's parking lot this elderly lady, going the wrong direction, cuts me off. I actually had to back up into the street so she could continue on her pathway which she refused to give up even though she was going in the wrong direction. She too was a driving an expensive car; a newish Mercedes.

Now, the guy, due to what he was driving, was probably a one-time or maybe a current high-end lawyer or doctor or something. He grew to be arrogant due to his life-position. The woman was probably the wife of someone who held high-stature so she too got bask in and embrace the pathway of arrogance. But, is arrogance ever a good thing? No, it is not. No matter how you get to that state, it is never a productive attitude. It hurts the life of others and it hurt the definition of you.

After all that, I drove to Trader Joe's on my way home to pick up a couple of salads and a baguette for a dinner and a few bottles of wine. As I always do, I bagged my own groceries. Cashiers have a hard enough life, and just like for everyone else, you need to make their journey just a little bit easier wherever you can.

Today, like always, the girl was so surprised when I started to bag my own groceries. They always thank me. But, they shouldn't have to. It should just be the way things are. People should do whenever they can do. They should try to make everyone's everything just a little bit easier. Why should that cashier have to bag my groceries while I stand there watching her when I have two hands and can do it just fine? Why should anyone sit back in a position of arrogance expecting things to be done for them?

In closing, never be arrogant. Yes, yes, I understand that arrogance is based, at least in part, upon a feeling of insecurity. If you are an insecure person and you allow it to project via a state of arrogance, stop it! Get yourself together! Get you mind together! Instead of trying to prove you are better than someone/anyone, get out there, eat your ego, and do good things for everyone. That has the potential to make everything better. Arrogance has the potential to make nothing better.

Here's an important thing to keep in mind, however, you can't fight arrogance because the only way you can prove you are better than that arrogant person is to be more arrogant than they are. Which is just the road to disaster. But, you can understand who and what that person is basing their reality upon, maybe even nudge them into following a more positive, helpful path. But, never go to battle with them because all that does is to allow them to embrace their arrogance even more. And, by doing so, (if you do so), you have allowed their arrogance to come to dominate your life. Do you want that? Do you want an arrogant person to be in control of you? Probably not.

Follow a life path of helpful humble goodness and meet arrogance with a smile.

* * *

06/Jan/2022 07:21 AM

Just because the liquid is clear and looks like water does not mean that it is water.

* * *

05/Jan/2022 10:02 AM

If you didn't know what day your birthday was on you wouldn't expect anyone to wish you a happy birthday.

Impermanence
04/Jan/2022 07:53 AM

The Sanskrit word for impermanence is, *"Aṅityātva."* In fact, there is an entire doctrine of thought devoted to the understanding of impermanence. It is named, *"Kṣaṇabhaṅguravāda."*

Here's the thing, it is very clear that all life is based upon impermanence. Though we all should understand and embrace this concept, that nothing is permanent, it seems we all fight this truth hoping to hold onto those things we care about and we love.

The things we care about and we love span the vast array of all life. Some of those things are people, some of those things are animal friends, some of those things are just things. But, think about it; think about those things that you love. You love them but the fact of the fact is, they are not going to last forever.

Have you ever has someone you cared about pass away. It pretty devastating, isn't it? You don't know until you know but when you do know you know.

But, people don't have to die to leave you. Maybe they just leave you and move on with their life. Heartbreaking.

Then there's the things… Those things that maybe no one else cares about but you do. Though you know their just things but you want them to last forever. Stupid maybe. But, you care about them and as you care about them you care about them.

I was looking through some production stills from a movie I did a decade ago or so. I noticed that my character was wearing these black and yellow New Balance tennis shoes. Though I had totally forgotten about those shoes, the moment I saw them in the photo I remembered how much I loved those shoes when I had them. I forget what actually happened to them but I guess like all things shoes-orientated they got old and they eventually died.

Seeing them made me wonder if I could get another pair and maybe live a little bit more of that feeling I had when I wore them way back in the way back when. I mean, I've been wearing the New Balance 992/993 series for decades and though they have evolved they are still available. Anyway, I did a quest. Nada. It looks like New Balance discontinued that model. I did see an old pair on eBay but they were trashed. It made me wonder who would buy an old, dead pair of tennis shoes for more than fifty bucks? Hey, maybe they're mine? Just joking, they weren't size twelve. So, I guess those shoes are gone forever. Sad...

I think back to this one pair of Pumas I used to have in the eighties. I kinda felt the same way about them. I remember I mentioned them in one of my novels, though I can't tell you exactly where but it was probably in, *The Passionate Kiss of Illusion*. They, like those New Balance, I really loved. Just so comfortable. Just so me at that point in history. But, they too are gone—long gone. Where or why, I also don't remember but like all things life, they just eventually disappeared.

Like the lyrics from the Yusuf Islam AKA Cat Stevens songs, *"Oh Very Young,"*

> *"Oh very young, what will you leave us this time*
> *You're only dancin' on this earth for a short while*
> *And though your dreams may toss and turn you now*
> *They will vanish away like your dads best jeans*
> *Denim blue, faded up to the sky*
> *And though you want them to last forever*
> *You know they never will*
> *(You know they never will)*
> *And the patches make the goodbye harder still."*

So, here's the thing, getting and having is grand. Sometimes/many times you don't know what you've got till it's gone. Oh crap, I just quoted another song. This one from Joni Mitchell... But, when you find those things, you fall in love with them.

Many things/most things are just there. Maybe you like them, maybe you don't, maybe they simply exist in your space of life. You use them but you don't really care about them. Then, there is those other things: those people, those pets, those musical instruments, those cars, those New Balance shoes, those whatever... For whatever reason, you really grow to love them. But, you gotta know they are going to go away.

Some things last longer than others. Some things (and/or people) may out last you—because you ain't permanent either. Sooner or later it's all gonna be gone: you me, those things we love, everything... I wish I could say there was a cure for this but there is not. All I can say is just prepare yourself, 'cause nothing last forever.

You can study the whole cause and effect of all of this in doctrines like the Kṣaṇabhaṅguravāda. But, the fact of the fact is, you just have to face the fact, nothing is permanent. Those shoes you love, they ain't gonna last forever.

Being Positive or Being Silent
03/Jan/2022 01:18 PM

Obviously, being positive is what I'm all about. It's my motto, *"Be Positive."*

Be Positive is in some ways a double entendre. One: Be Positive: Be a positive person who says and does positive things. Two: Be Positive: Make sure that what you believe and what you are speaking, based upon what you believe, is factually correct.

Think about it… How few people base their lives upon this perspective. My guess is, very few.

I believe if we look around at life, very few people base their life upon being positive. Everything they do is emotion, belief, and desire based. Just look around at the events of the world over the past couple of years; it's nuts! You don't have to look too far to see major upheaval. Is any of that based in positivity?

Look around your own life and your own life surroundings—even at the local level, so much is going on. Again, it's nuts! How much of what you personally encounter is based upon positivity?

Let's take a look at all of this from a personal perspective. How much of what you do is based upon positivity? What percentage of your actions are based upon achieving a positive result?

Many people confuse what they believe or what they want as a pathway to positivity. But, is it? Isn't that just an individual's desires being broadcast outwards to the world?

This is where many/most of the problems of the world begin: an individual wanting something, an individual doing something that they want to do, an individual believing something and then basing their actions upon that belief. But is any of that true positivity? Is something positive simply because (maybe) you have gotten what you wanted?

If you look to your own life, what in it is positive? Truly take a moment and chart out those things. What is positive in your life and why is it positive? What got you to that positivity? Were the actions you took that got you there all positive or was there some negativity involved. Be honest with yourself. If there was any negativity involved, then ask yourself, how can you base positivity upon negativity? Can you?

Now, flip this around. What is negative in your life? What caused that negativity? How were you personally involved in creating that negativity? What have you done to countermand, correct, or undo that negativity? And, if you have unleashed negativity onto the life of someone/anyone else, do you even care? If you do, what have you done to correct what you have instigated? Ultimately, positivity or negativity begins with you.

These are all things that most people never even think about. They just do what they do, want what they want, feel what they feel, believe what they believe, and don't care about the process as long as they get what they want whenever they are wanting it. How about you? Do you care about what your wanting, equally your doing, does to your life, to the life other people, and to this life-space on the whole?

As we all base our life understandings upon what we have lived, I too base my life understandings upon those things. When I look out to the world, I see that a lot of people have been very kind to me. I get positive messages from positive people all the time. Some ask me questions, some want to hang out, some ask me to give a talk, teach a class, or do a seminar, some just want to wish me well. Great! Thank you! Keep the positivity spreading!

On the flip side of this, due to the fact that at least a small portion of my life has been lived in the public eye, I have also received random acts of negativity. There have been mean and hurtful comments made about me, false speculations and ideas put out there, and unfounded criticisms unleashed. There have even been a few lies that have been told about me. I'm sure you have experienced things like that in your life, as well. So, you know the feeling.

Thankfully, I've encounter only a small amount of those life-things but some of them are still out there to this day. When I have received those attacks, what I have witnessed is how few people, who have extended positivity in my direction, say or do anything. They just let it stand. They're silent. On the other hand, when I have been forced to stand up for myself, then I get hit with a ton of negativity. This, for me standing up for my rights and/or the truth. Interesting…

We all can understand how negativity is a much more powerful emotion than positivity as it drives one's adrenaline. But, that does not make it a good thing. Negativity is never positivity. It is never a good thing.

What I find is that so many truly positive people are very quiet in their positivity. They may embrace positivity. They may live a positive lifestyle. They may emulate positivity. But, they are silent in their spreading of that positivity. Though understandable, there is a problem in all of this.

How much time do you spend being silent—not being involved? Yes, in your moment you may like someone or something, you may think positive thoughts about them, you may say positive things about them in the company of your friends, but how often do you reach out to that person or that thing with a gesture of positivity? How much positive aid do you provide for that person you have never met or that thing you have never personally experienced when you witness some negativity being guided in their direction?

Silence is easy. Silence is safe. Silence keeps you from confrontation. But, silence never sets anything right.

I do not endorse or encourage attacking anyone or anything on any level. In fact, I'm totally against it. But, if you people who do base your life upon positivity do nothing to countermand negativity; who and what wins? If you do not add positivity to the equation of negativity, who and what wins? As you have done nothing to countermand negativity, negativity reigns supreme.

Again, look around the world… How much of what is taking place, on the personal or the global level, is based in positivity and how much of it based upon negativity?

What I'm saying here is, first of all, base your life upon positivity. As we all understand, positivity is just better. But, more than that, don't become a part of the negative express. If you see or hear someone saying or doing something negative; meet that action with you saying or doing something based in positivity. Meet criticism with praise. Meet anger with peace. Meet negativity with positivity.

It's you who can make a difference in this world. It's you who can cause an entire shift in the conversation by presenting positivity whenever anyone is locked into the negative. Choose to be proactive in your positivity. Believe me, everything will become better.

Be Positive and Smile.

Mind Games
02/Jan/2022 07:56 AM

Ever since the dawning of humanity and the desire for deeper understanding and rising human consciousness there have been those false prophets who take to the stage and attempt to gain followers as a means to not only make money but to gain control over others to fulfill that empty something within themselves as they guide people down some path that they believe they should follow. In other words, there are a lot of liars out there who lay claim to being a, *"Knower."*

This so-called, *"Knowing,"* is fueled by other people's desire to know. As something is missing in their life—as they have lost a loved one and want to know why, as they have unanswered questioned about the road to realization they are on or their general pathway in life they look to those people who claim to know. But, do these people know or are they simply a lair or an individual who lies to themselves?

As I have long said, the best way to test any so-called psychic is to ask them a question about yourself or your family lineage that they would have no way of knowing the answer to—something that they cannot look up on the internet or deduct from what you wear or how you behave.

I remember back to the first time I traveled to India. I had just arrived and was walking around the marketplace in Delhi. One of those many so-called psychics, who mingled around the area back then, came up to me and did what all the sellers in that market do—they targeted someone and will not let them go until they get some money out of them. This guy was pretending to go into some trance and was telling me I had come to India to find enlightenment. He knew that fact, but I could only find it if I gave him some rupees as that is what my spiritual guru, in the ethereal realm, wanted me to do. Are you kidding me! I mean, come on!

There I was, a white guy with long hair and a beard, wearing yogi clothing and prayer beads in the marketplace in Delhi, why would anyone think I was there? It was pretty obvious. Finally, I gave him a few rupees so he would leave me alone. Or, maybe it made my spiritual guru happy.

But, here's the things and the other side to all of this... Some people actually believe that they, *"Know."* For example, earlier on that same journey, I was at LAX. This was a time in history when there were all kinds of sales people roaming the airports, spiritual and otherwise. Thankfully, they have all now been banned; well, at least, the most obvious of them.

Anyway, this Hare Krishna girl came up to me and tried to sell me a book composed by her teacher, Swami Prabhupada Bhaktivedanta. Back then, Hare Krishnas were everywhere. They were dancing on the corners of the streets in the major cities and they would try to recruit you and sell you books and stuff like that all the time. Even me, I had gone to their temple over in Culver City a couple of times, just to find out the what's what.

The thing is, they were so flamboyant they became almost a joke—a punch line in a joke. But, were they wrong in their belief? No. They were true believers. So, were they wrong in what they believed? No. Were they wrong in trying to convert and bring people to their way of believing? No. How is any Christian any different? This is the thing, some people want to believe. Some people need something to believe in. And, here lies one of the main impetuses for the problem in all of this. Some people need to believe and they need to be feed the what they believe in by someone else.

To finish the/this storyline... The girl at LAX eventually told me, in no uncertain terms, *"I was a fool,"* because I rejected her teaching, stating that I was on my way to India to follow the true pathway, etc... Was I a fool? Maybe. Was she? Maybe. Where is she now? Where am I now? And, who really know the truth of the truth?

To continue, in my life I have met a lot of false profits. ...A lot of people who were really lost, ego-driven people, claiming they knew something that others did not know. I have also met a number of truly psychologically disturbed people who claimed that they had some mystical gift that others did not possess. Some sold this so-called gift. They claimed they could go into a trance and communicate with that whomever or whatever out there in the cosmos. Some even claimed to be the singular channel for some great spiritual being. Now, I could say they were all full of bullshit and you would probably agree. But, would that change their mind? Though they may not be able to get some money or some worship out of you or me, as that is what they are seeking, would that make them change what they do? Probably not.

Just like I say, ask a psychic something that they cannot know about you to prove to you and to them that they are not what they claim, I also say, if someone says that they have this great power to communicate with some spiritual essence from the great beyond ask them, *"Let's see it."* Make them present it to you right there.

Now, I'm not talking about those people that spew out gibberish and claim to be in some trance. That's just bullshit anyone can pretend to do with some practice. I'm saying, make them present that energy in physical form. Sure, they will make a ton of excuses about why they can't do that and why you should believe them anyway. But, if they can't, they can't, and because they can't that proves to you the definition of who and what they truly are.

Whenever you look to a teacher for spiritual or life guidance, you really need to look deeply into who and what that person truly is and why they are doing what they are doing and mostly what they are getting out of what they do. For example, I remember after my shrink had retired, for a couple of session I went to another one. My original shrink was truly a good person. In fact, due to the fact I was going through some financial challenges, at one point in time, she didn't even charge me for my sessions. Can you believe that? A shrink who does their job for free. That is a person truly trying to help for no other reason but to help. This other shrink, however, was not about that. What I realized, after my years-upon-years of reading and studying all the writings and ideas of psychology, was that I knew way more than her. She had nothing to offer me. Yet, after I said, *"Bye-bye,"* she would call me and call me trying to get me and my hundred dollars a session back. But, I never went back.

What I am saying is that people may claim to be an aid or a guide to you in many ways—they may come at you from many directions. Some you may even seek out and contact yourself. But, you must be honest with yourself—you must make them prove who and what they truly are and why they are doing what they are doing. Because if you don't, you allow them to exist in the world of Mind Games, where they get whatever it is they need and/or want out of you and out of life, while you pay the freight. In other words, be careful whom you turn to for the truth because, most likely, they do not possess it.

* * *
02/Jan/2022 07:55 AM

It's important to be honest with yourself and understand the things that you don't do well so you don't try to do them and do them badly.

Let's Be More Considerate
31/Dec/2021 02:16 PM

Ever since the close-downs ended with this current pandemic, and people started to take back to the streets, I believe it has become fairly obvious that people have become very-very self-centered. Whatever is the basis of their self-centeredness is anyone's guess but that is what they have become. One would think that it should have gone in the other direction; that people would have realized that they need to care more about one another. But, that has not been the case.

Here were are at the end of 2021. Whenever the new year comes people always seem to make those New Years Resolutions. Those too are generally a very self-centered ideology. They want something to become more or better for themselves. Those hopes are fine but it does not have to be that way—it does not have to be all about you.

Tomorrow will be 2022, why don't we all, instead of only thinking about ourselves, consciously choose to become more considerate: more considerate of the people we know, more considerate of the people we don't know, more considerate of the all and the everyone and the everything.

All life begins with you. All life has the potential of becoming better because of you. All life has the chance to be changed by you. Why don't you begin this process by being more considerate; caring and thinking more about the other person instead of only thinking about yourself. Let's be more considerate.

Just Because You Do Yoga That Does Not Make You a Yogi
30/Dec/2021 08:28 AM

As I have passed through my life, periodically I have witnessed when there were times when yoga rose to the center stage and many people became practitioners. Yes, there were some who truly understood the true nature of what yoga is but most never did.

I would think that yoga probably had its first rapid rise to modern notoriety, at least here in the West, in the 1960s. Though certainly referenced in western literature long before this period of time, I do not believe that it truly grabbed hold until the time of the rise of the counterculture. I know this is the era when I found my way to yoga.

As a young child, who was a latch key kid, long before that term was ever invented, I would watch a man named Richard Hittleman on PBS and practice the techniques of yoga and meditation guided by him. That early schooling never left me and throughout my childhood and early adolescence I would seek out more information about what yoga truly was.

By the 1970s, yoga was everywhere. There were numerous books on the subject. There were centers that taught the various aspects of yoga all across the globe. At sixteen, when I got a car and could drive, this is where I began my association with Swami Satchidananda's Integral Yoga Institute. Prior to owning a car it was difficult for me to seek out and investigate the various spiritual centers around L.A. It was at the Integral Yoga Institute that I was truly ushered into the true practice and meaning of yoga.

The understanding of what yoga truly is becomes the break point for absolute comprehension of this spiritual science and provides one with the ability to delve deeper into one's self and the truth of yoga.

Many people, when they hear the term, *"Yoga,"* immediately associate it with the physical aspects of yoga. But, those are actually known as, *"Hatha Yoga,"* which is a very small part of the overall science of yoga. When you tell people what the term, *"Yoga,"* actually means, *"Union with god,"* and how it is based in Hinduism and possesses a Hindu understanding of reality; some may argue this point, some refuse to believe it, others simply dismiss it. But, the fact of the fact is, what yoga truly embodies is understood by very few modern practitioners.

Yoga has come to be embraced by different generations in somewhat different ways since it was introduced to the West. I think back to this girl I came to know, who was a server at a restaurant I used to frequent. We got to speaking a lot and it turned out she was a recovering crack addict and her mother, who was also in the process of recovery, ended up becoming initially involved in yoga via the postures which later lead her to move to the ashram of Baba Hari Dass near Santa Cruz, California. Her daughter, my friend, dismissed all of the emersion of her mother into the true techniques of yoga but liked to practice the postures; though she never did one of the most elemental parts of all branches of yoga, embracing a healthy body. She never stopped smoking.

There was also a male server at this restaurant that I came to know, as well, during this same period of time. It was one of those things that she was into me, but he was into her, so it was a little weird. Due to his being into her, he went with her to the hatha yoga classes but completely rebuked the meditation segment of the class as, *"Bullshit."* But, he liked the stretching of the yoga postures.

Time went on. I would go back into the restaurant where I found my female friend to be tweaking again. You can see it in their eyes and witness it in their behavior. Eventually they were both gone. Did the yoga help them? Maybe? Did it save her from drug addiction? No. But, was she actually practicing yoga or simply going through the physical motions? Again, there is a large difference between the physical postures associated with yoga and true yoga.

I think back to a conversation I had with a couple of extended female family members, who were both very much into, *"Yoga,"* a couple of years ago. Again, during another period of time when yoga was highly embraced by the masses… I got to talking to them about the true meaning of yoga but all they could say was, *"Let's see you do what every hatha yoga posture they called up."* *"That's not yoga,"* I exclaimed. *"Yoga is a pathway towards union with god."* But, more than that, my body is so torn up from my decades upon decades of involvement with the martial arts that my hatha yoga postures could not be performed with any grand level of excellence anymore.

Speaking of the martial arts, this is a <u>something</u> that is similar in yoga. In the martial arts, there are some people who develop into great technicians. Some do not. Though all can learn and practice the various techniques, some simply excel in their beauty. This is the same with the physical aspects of yoga.

Many years ago, when I was still in high school, one of the Swamis from the Integral Yoga Institute asked me to go and give a hatha yoga demonstration with him at a high school in West Los Angeles. I was happy to do it. He gave the talk, because he felt I did the postures better than he. At the time, I always thought that was strange. There I was a novice doing the postures in front of the class. There he was, a Swami wanting a novice to demonstrate the techniques. Shouldn't he do them better than I?

This takes us to the point of the point of all of this. Yes, hatha yoga is a branch of yoga. But, it is only a physical brand of yoga. To the true yogi, it is one of the lowest levels of yoga as it is <u>only</u> physical. True yoga is about a person's emersion into the spiritual realms of consciousness. It is about leaving the physical body behind. Though hatha yoga may be a gateway of introducing a person to yoga, it is never the end-point. As it is physical, it is only physical. Doing the physical postures of yoga is not a pathway to god or enlightenment. At best, it is a meditative practice which allows the practitioner to come to master their body.

Here lies the conundrum in all of this. Many hatha yoga practitioners become ego-filled with the fact that they can do the postures with some level of excellence. But, ego is the pathway to nothing more than self-embellishment. It is not the pathway to god or enlightenment. So, the next time you encounter a person who proclaims their prowess in yoga—perhaps someone who hopes to teach you yoga, ask them what yoga truly is. If all they have for an answer is the physical postures or some breathing or meditation techniques to offer you, you can clearly understand that they do not know what, *"Yoga,"* actually mean.

Interpretations Based on Lies
29/Dec/2021 08:33 AM

Whenever I am referenced in regard to my films, it is virtually inevitable that people speak about *The Roller Blade Seven* and *Max Hell Frog Warrior*. I guess, over time, those films have proven to be the most rememberable. But, I have made a lot more films and documentaries than simply those two.

Whenever I am referenced in regard to my films, it is virtually inevitable that people attempt to speculate what my mindset was and/or is in regard to filmmaking and why I did what I did. But, they are virtually always wrong.

Whenever I am referenced in regard to my films, it is virtually inevitable that people attempt to cast their judgment onto those films, speak their mind about how I did what I did, why I did what I did, how what I did was wrong, and how by doing what I did equaled a bad film. Though opinions are one of the greatest gifts to modern man (and woman) kind, they are not based in fact. They are guesswork at best. Thus, in all I have heard or read, no-one even comes close to understanding the truth about what actually took place or why it equaled the outcome that it did.

Whenever I am references in regard to my films, it is virtually inevitable that the person doing the speaking (or the writing) has never spoken to me. This has always perplexed me immensely. Why does no one ask me? Don't you think if you want the truth of the truth you go to the source? Yet, all of this proclaiming goes on but not one of the people doing the proclaiming has ever interacted with me on a personal level. Don't you see the problem in that?

I forever wonder, *"Don't people feel bad when they are saying something that is not true?"* If I can answer my own question, I guess the answer to that question is, *"No."* But, why is what they are stating wrong? Answer: Because they never really take the time to truly research and learn the facts and they certainly never go back and retract any statement they make once that statement has proven to be incorrect.

The reason I go into all this today, (and there is nothing new in any of this), is the fact that everyone who writes or talks about my films or myself presume that they know something; some secret and unknown thing that should be revealed to the masses. But, they are wrong in virtually all that they proclaim. Again, don't you see the problem in that?

I came to the film game relatively late in life. I was in my early thirties. But, when I did, I dove straight in. Like many who get into acting, I initially had dreams of red carpets and stardom. This, even though I grew up in Hollywood, California and had, up until that point in time, completely rebuked the industry. But, after numerous offers, my curiosity got peaked and I tried to grab the golden ring. I had some small success. But, it seem my destiny called me into another direction.

Here's the thing, if you wish to, *"Make it,"* in Hollywood, and I used that term, "Hollywood," as a greater whole, you must constantly rely on someone else's judgment of you. *"Are you right for the role?" "Do you have the right look?" "Will your name mean anything to the sales of the production?" "Will you give the producer sex?"* A question I said, *"No,"* to more than once. #metoo.

All this being said, what I found was that if you produced your own films, you could constantly work. You could make cinematic art. But, back then, when I first entered the filmmaking game, and even today, making that cinematic art was and is not cheap. But, if you could get some money for some equipment, production and post production costs then, *"Yes,"* you could make a movie. Which is what I did.

Somebody asked me about one of Donald G. Jackson's films, *Roller Blade Warriors* this morning, which set me to thinking about all of this… As I have stated in the past, when Don asked me to work with him, I had never seen any of his films. I was into a completely different style of filmmaking. One day, when we had just begun doing *Roller Blade Seven,* we were at an actress's house in West Hollywood, and Don pops in a copy of *Roller Blade Warrior* into the video deck. I was shocked at its horribleness. Though it did cost upwards of a million dollars to make. My first thought was to leave and never look back but I made the choice, perhaps the wrong choice, not to leave. Thus, my work with him has come to be, at least part, of my filmmaking legacy. We made a lot of film together. Some people like them, some do not. But, what actually is like and dislike? Isn't it only a person placing their own predetermined definitions onto what they believe is good or what they think is bad?

As thirty years or so have progressed since that fateful day when Don and I began creating our first film together; me, personally, I have made a lot of films. In fact, I had made a few films before that point in time when I met DGJ. But, what any filmmaker is define by, whether rightly or wrongly, is the interpretation of the viewer. If a filmmaker allows that to define their pathway, however, then all that is created is done so simply as a means of appeasement to the viewer and is never a true representation of what the filmmaker has envisioned in their mind. Me, I have always believed that art is art and art can only be defined in the mind of the artist. Yes, some art comes to be liked or loved more than other art but that does not take its essence away. In fact, think about it, more art is never seen than is seen. How many artists have created art, through the history of humanity, that was lost to the eyes of the viewer and was never seen at all?

As art is art and as art is all about the artist creating the art and the viewer viewing the art, then all art, by its very definition, is a process of personal interpretation. And, personal interpretation, by its very nature, is based upon bias.

This being said, and perhaps one of the keys to living a life of understanding instead of a life defined by prejudice, is to understand that your interpretation is only your interpretation—your appraisal is only your appraisal. If you attempt to spout your appraisal to the world than what you have done is to cause others to either believe your words or disbelieve what you are saying. But, by behaving in this fashion, what you have done is to remove personal exploration; not only of any artwork but of the depth of an individual's own personality, as well. You have halted their developing understanding of what they truly do or do not believe because you have interceded with your thoughts which are not necessarily their thoughts.

In life—in all life, everything is defined by individual interpretation. But, if you cast your interpretation into the mind's of others, you have taken away their ability to form their own understanding. If, when you do this, you do so by presenting falsehood as your premise, then you have created a world based upon the lies that you have told. What do you think is the ultimate ramifications of that?

In closing, think what you want to think and be who you want to be. But remember, if you feel your interpretation of art, or any other realm of life science, is worthy of being listening to by the masses, at least be right in your dissemination. If not, all you have done is to help create a world based upon lies.

* * *
27/Dec/2021 07:55 AM

Every gift comes with a price tag.

Let's Meet Up
26/Dec/2021 07:59 AM

Ever since the birth of this pandemic, people have been kept from meeting one another. Also, since the birth of this pandemic, people have found unique ways to keep relationships alive.

Back when we were told that we were to be no closer that six-feet away from one another, I would see people pulling their SUVs back-to-back in parking lots where the occupants would sit on their rear decks, six feet apart, to have their conversations. I always found that amusing.

As time has gone on, we learned that as long as we are outdoors, and not directly in each other's faces, it is probably okay if we communicate. With this, people have come to use other and new means to meet. For example, there is this one shopping center, not too far from where I live. Every time I go there on a Saturday, there is this group of elderly men who are sitting in the parking lot, surrounded by their cars, in their fold-out chairs, having what I guess is their weekly meeting. I don't know? A parking lot just does not seem all that appealing of a location for a weekly meeting. Why don't they go to a park or something? But, to each their own…

There is also this guy, I periodically see, in this other shopping center parking lot. When I go there he is sometimes parked over in one corner. He sits there in a fold-out chair, with his dog on a leash, in front of his '66 Mustang. Again, why a parking lot?

I think back to the time, pre-pandemic… I have a couple of actor friends. They are fairly well-known guys. They would sit-down at this restaurant or that and order a coffee. There, they would sit, sometimes all day, holding court with all of those wanna-be friends and foes who hoped they would usher them into the industry. These restaurants would eventually tell them to leave as they were taking up the table space for far too long. Then, they moved onto the next and the next location.

I don't know? I've just never been one of those people who likes small talk. It just seems pointless. I find if conversation lags with a person or if I have to think about something to say or force myself to talk with them we really don't have that much in common. And, I hate to dive into those conversations, with long-time friends, about the what once was, way back in the way back when.

I do love coffee houses and locations like Starbucks, however. I go to them all the time. They are a great place to solo hang out and ponder life or to meet and talk.

One upon a time, here in the L.A. area, there were pretty much none of those style of locations left. The '60s coffee house were gone and until the '80, when a few pâtisseries began to open up, there was no place like that. Then came the wave of Starbucks and Coffee Bean and Tea Leafs. You see people bringing in their laptops and hanging out for hours-upon-hours. I don't know how some of those places make a profit with people taking possession of the tables and only buying one small drink.

Some of the locations have left us, however. I first began to notice this, many years ago now, when this Starbucks location that I really liked in Hong Kong packed up and was gone. I flew back into the city and headed over there the next AM but no more; they were gone. This trend really amplified during the pandemic. A lot of the under-performing locations have closed; including my favorite local haunt. But, that's life… If you don't change with the change you never change.

All this brings us to the point of the point—the need for human interaction and communication. We need to meet. Who do you meet? Where do you meet? What does your meeting give to you and what does your meeting do to and for that other person? What does it do to and for the location where you meet?

The all and the everything of the everything is, everything you do has consequences. It has consequences to you, it has consequences to them, and it has consequences to the greater all of the everything. If you don't ponder this, if you don't consciously consider this, if you don't take that next person, that you do not even know, who may observing and/or be affected by your convergence into consideration, then all you have done is to bring two or more personal energies together for very selfish reasons.

What do your meetings with others equal? Why do you meet? If you don't meet, why are you alone—why do you allow yourself to be alone? And, how does your alone impact the location where other people meet in couples or larger groups?

All life is based upon human interaction. From meeting to talking; from doing to having babies. What contribution does your meeting with others give to the all and the everything of the universal truth of existence? If you don't know, you don't know. If you don't contemplate this, you can never know?

Know why you do what you do. Know why you meet the people you meet. By knowing this, the all of your meeting(s) becomes based in something more than nothing. From this knowing, your meeting(s) can mean something more than simply the killing of time until you die.

Didn't See That One Coming
24/Dec/2021 04:16 PM

Life is full of surprises. Hopefully most of the surprises in your life will be positive. Hopefully good things will come your way.

Though we can all hope that we, and those we know and care about, will encounter good things in their life, sometimes things come out of nowhere and take us by surprise—things that we do not want to happen. Maybe it is that flat tire. No big deal but just one of those hassles that you would prefer not to have to deal with. Then, there are those bigger things. Maybe someone verbally attacks you, tells a lie about you, or something like that. Maybe someone breaks your heart. Maybe someone runs into your car. Recently, here in the L.A. area, there have been a bunch of strong-armed robberies taking place. People will be eating outside at a restaurant, or they will be followed home and someone will come up, stick a gun in their face, and take their watch, their jewelry, their purse, or their money. These are all really negative things that can leave lasting impressions on a person. ...Never expected or desired but they come out of the blue.

In life, it really comes down to one thing: good is always good and bad is forever bad. Like I have long said, if you love Hell it becomes Heaven but most people do not possess the refined mindset to redefine individual experiences and transition the bad into the good. They just feel what they feel when they feel it.

What do you do when something unexpected comes your way? Really ponder this question for a moment. For each of us it is different. But, do you ever take the time to truly evaluate what you are feeling or how you are reacting when a situation is occurring—when the positive and/or the negative surprisingly comes your way?

Have you ever had one of those experiences where you, all of a sudden, realized that you are having a really good time? Or maybe, you begin to eat a meal and you realized that what you are eating is really-really good. But, almost as soon as you realized this, your meal is over—the experience had culminated. You knew it was good but now that good is gone. Then what?

The things is, we all have the tenancy to become lost in our experiences: be they good or be they bad. Most of life is pretty commonplace but then there are those experiences that are something more.

For some, they must encounter badness brought on by those around them. Maybe they are attack: verbally or physically. Maybe someone unconsciously does something like causes them to have car accident. Or maybe, someone targets them.

Here's the thing, people who focus on the life of someone else and intentionally say bad things about an individual or do bad things to anyone are living their life from the very sad perspective of outside focus. They concentrate on someone else because what they are feeling or what they are doing with their own life holds no true worth. Even for those robbing others, they do this to get what that other person has. Thus, as they are empty in their own life, they are drawn to the life of someone else. From this, they seek to hurt other people or appear to be more than that other person either through words or via physical actions. Think about it… When someone has hurt you, why did they do it? Or, when you have hurt someone, why did you do it?

Most people never contemplate any of this. They just become lost in the experience of the experience. If it is good; great. If it is bad; not great. But, where is any refined understanding in any of this?

Lower-level people may attempt to hurt you. Why they do that is anyone's guess, but the fact of the fact is, there are people like that out there. At some point in your life, you may encounter someone with this mindset. There are also the really good people out there. People who will help you and/or give to you, (or anyone else), for no better reason than that is what they do.

Who are you? Which one of these levels of consciousness do you exist upon? More importantly, did you/do you choose to be who and what you are? Or, do you simply allow your lower level of undefined emotions to guide you on pathway where you leave hurt in your wake?

Let's go back to when someone surprisingly does something negative to you for a moment. In the past, how have you reacted? Did you allow their actions to take control over you? Or, did you refuse to allow them to control the inner you? Did you reframe the event into a learning experience that lead you towards your betterment? Or, did you allow it to destroy you?

If you take a true look at what other people do to you, you will see that though you may not be able to stop or undo what they have done, what you can do is to redefine the event by your own standards and move it to a higher level of learning. You can make the bad into good if you choose to possess the mental perspective to do so.

This is not necessarily easy. And, it never involves revenge or re-hurt. Because all that does is to further give control to the person who instigated the pain. It makes you become the badness they initiated.

Though this higher level of redefinition is not easy, it is doable. And, by doing this—by transitioning their bad into something good, not only have you taken control over their negative doing(s), you have proven to be the better person to anyone who is watching.

What about the times you have hurt someone? I'm sure that came at them with a surprise. Why did you do it? Did you do it consciously? Did you do it intentionally? Did you truly study your motivations before you did it? Or, did you do it simply because you could?

If you hurt anyone for any reason, you hurt someone. That is now the definition of your life. That is now proof that you are not a good or a worthy person. What are you going to do about that fact? Lie to yourself? Lie to others? Pretend you did nothing? Act like you don't care? If you do any of those things, nothing becomes any better. All you are is just another person who did another bad thing adding to the non-goodness that is out there.

All life begins with you. I say this all the time. If someone hurts you, it is what you do next with that experience that sets the stage for the rest of your life. If you hurt someone else, it is what you do next with that experience that sets the stage for the rest of your life.

Though much of life is out of our control—it comes at us in a flash we never expected, what is in your control is what you do with the cards you have been deal. It is what you do to others which will define what they will do to and for you.

Choose to be in control of your life no matter what the circumstances. Though things may come at you that you never expected: both good and bad, be in the moment with those occurrences and transcend above all of them to the most positive place they can be elevated to.

Mostly, be that person who does that something nice for that someone else. Maybe you know them, maybe you don't, but we all remember those good things done by those nice people. Let that be the memory you leave with everyone. Let that be the life surprise you give to them.

Hypocrisy
23/Dec/2021 10:43 AM

Ever since the dawning of the COVID-19 pandemic, all of our lives have been changed. Though there were hopes and dreams that it would be gone by this point in time, it doesn't look like it is going away any time soon.

From this pandemic, we have all been driven into a new reality. This reality has forced us to shift our understanding away from simply the Self and onto the needs and the existence of others. For some, they have stepped up to the plate and truly devoted themselves to helping their fellow human beings. For others, they have simply used this pandemic as a means to reinvigorate and to spout their beliefs about how life should be lived onto others.

I could quote all kinds of biblical passages about what could be described a predictions of this pandemic in the Bible. But, I am certain all of the Christian pundits have already done that. What I will say is that, this pandemic has truly shown us the true nature of humanity. It has illustrated the goodness of some people and the self-centeredness of others.

Since the development of the COVID-19 vaccines, which occurred amazingly quickly, some people have linked them to all kinds of conspiracy theories and refused to get vaccinated. I respect everyone's believe and the right to do what they believe is right for them. And, I am not trying to stir up anybody's anger. But, there is something much more at play here then what a person does or does not want to do with their own body. There is the entire spectrum of humanity that can be affected by one person's choice not to get vaccinated. If they get the disease, they may spread it to others and from this that other person may die. This happened to my mother-in-law. COVID-19 was given to her by her unvaccinated son; who still has not be vaccinated. She died. He killed her. What is the karma in that?

But, more to the point, at least to the point of this piece. I was watching the BBC last night and Dr. Leana Wen, who is one of those talking head doctors frequently featured on networks like CNN and the BBC, in regard to this pandemic. She is also a graduate of one of my alma maters, California State University, Los Angeles. But, she began her attendance there when she was thirteen. I was much older. Anyway... She said something very profound. She stated that it is hypocritical for the people who refuse to be vaccinated but then when they contract COVID-19 to immediately rush to the hospitable willing to take any medical cure they can be given. Have you thought about that? ...Especially those of you who refuse to get a COVID-19 vaccination. It is hypocrisy.

There are certain religions where they refuse all types of medical treatment. They believe that god and prayer is enough. That's their belief and as long as they stand by it they cannot be criticized. Though their logic may be questioned? Then, there is all of the everyone else. Those people that, for lack of a better term, politicize their beliefs— particularly in regard to this pandemic.

They way I see life is that, yes, we are all individuals. But, what we do in our life not only affects us but has the potential to affect so many others. This is especially true in this pandemic. It is not all about you!

So, if you refuse to get vaxed that's your choice. But, you may kill someone else. Meaning, that was your choice as well and you will have to live with and suffer the consequences. As was so aptly stated by Dr. Wen, if you refuse to get vaxed then you should not go to a hospitable and expect to be cured if your do contract COVID-19 because that makes you a hypocrite.

You know... You can care about humanity. You can take the focus off of your Self. Or, you don't. Your life. Your choice. But, if you don't care about the All and the

Everything more than simply thinking about YOU, how do you expect the evolutionary karma of your life will unfold?

As I say over and over again, CARE! That is the ultimate gift you can give to anyone.

When You Hurt Someone
22/Dec/2021 01:19 PM

When you hurt someone, you hurt someone, and that is the end of the story. Many people falsely believe that they have the right to hurt someone. Maybe they feel that person said something or did something and they deserve to be hurt for it. But, think about it, who has the right to hurt anyone—especially if that person did nothing directly to the person who is unleashing the pain?

Ever since we entered this era of Cancel Culture, everyone is being called out for everything. Somebody didn't like what someone else said or did and BAM let's go after them! But, what happens from this style of behavior? Does the person doing the attacking ever think about this? Most likely, no. They just attacked. But, what becomes the consequences of that action? What happens next is that someone gets hurt. Then what? Answer: A whole ton of bad karma is created.

Here's the facts, just because you think you have the right to speak out against someone does not mean that there will not be consequences. And, I am not speaking about someone counterattacking you, though that may very well come to pass. What I am speaking about is that by hurting anyone, you have set a whole plethora of bad energy into motion.

Keep in mind, just because you believe you are right, does not mean that you are right. Just because you believe that someone else is wrong, does not mean that they are wrong. Hate speech is never free speech.

I talk about this all the time, but people throw shots at other people anonymously, via some screen name, on the internet. Why? Because they feel there will be no repercussions. But, is life truly that simple?

Maybe they don't like what that person stands for. They may not like what they have said. They may like what they did. They may not like <u>whatever</u> about that person. But, all that is formed in personality-based Mind Stuff. It is not based in the Truth. It is simply based in perception and this is why doing anything framed by that mindset equals bad karma. Do you ever think about this?

In recently times a lot of people have been, *"Cancelled."* Certainly some of those on forefront of attacks have been comedians. Certain people don't like their humor. Personally, I've never really been a fan of stand-up comedy. It's just not what I'm into. That being said, I understand that comedy is about the framing of human reality in a very specific manner and sometimes that means it uses personal or cultural attacks as a means to get a laugh. Via words, it causes the listener to reexamine and rethink certain things in a different than expected manner. Sometimes comedy involves attack on a specific subject matter. But, where comedy differs from a personal attack is that it is designed to create laughter. In some cases, this is achieved via sarcasm. Yet, look at how many comedians have been thought to now be Politically Incorrect for saying something that they've said for years.

Sure, all this Cancel-Stuff this can be looked at as a time for change and reexamination. But, if anyone is hurt, if anyone is attacked by anyone, where do you think that karma lies? It goes straight to the life of those who are doing the hurting.

All you have to do is watch the life of a person who attacks others over a period of time and you will clearly see that they are not living a good or a truly fulfilled and happy existence. They are, at best, driven by anger and distain, which causes them to lead an adrenalized life. But, is that any way to live? Is that living a good life?

The thing about life is, you can explain to someone that what they are doing is not good, but if they don't listen to you, your words mean nothing. Moreover, each person is doomed to live their own destiny, created, in no small part, by what they say to others and about others and how they behave in relation to others on the grand-scale of life.

Let's take this to the personal level. Think about a time when you said something negative about a person based upon how you felt about something they said or did. Yes, you may have felt invigorated by that expression of your feelings. Yes, maybe even some people cheered you on. But, what happened next in your life? What happened later on down the road of your life? Did good things come to you because of what you said or did? Or, did your life begin to languish in the mundane or even the negative? Most likely, the ladder is true.

I've never seen a person yet who lived an ongoing happy and fulfilled life who based their existence upon a negative attack on a person or persons or a life based upon their negative appraisal of the all and the everybody.

Attack equals hurt. Hurt equals retribution. And, retribution comes out of nowhere when you never expect it. It may come in a day, it may come in a year, it may come in a decade, but it will come.

What I am saying here is, if you think your attack on someone, based upon what you do not like in them, is going to equal anything good in your life, think again. It will not.

Though karma is an accepted word to describe the repercussions a person experiences due to what they have done to someone else, it is just a word. Negative doing equals negative doing. If you say or do something negative, that hurts the life of someone else, you will have instigated that negativity and, due to your own instigation, it has already been brought into your own life. You will pay the price.

In closing, we all think what we think about other people. That's natural. We like what some people say and do, we don't like what others say or do. That's also natural. But, the moment you decide you are judge and jury for anyone; game over. If you bring negativity to the life of anyone, you have instigated that negativity and you will encounter its backlash. It is for this reason that I always say, meet negativity with positivity. Seek to see the goodness in everyone. Even if you don't like someone, don't call them out on it just because you can. Try to find the good in what they do. Focus on that good. Even proclaim that good. Then, good is all you will have created and that good will come to find you.

* * *
21/Dec/2021 01:35 PM

If you don't wash your cup it will always remain dirty.

Sitting on the Sidewalk with a Smile on Their Face
21/Dec/2021 12:45 PM

I think every community has those outliers of people. Those ones who are a little different. Those people that appear to be a little strange. I know mine does.

Where I live there are a lot of people of Asian and Middle Eastern descent. Due to this fact, these are the kind of people I see and interact with all the time. As such and because of, these are also some of the people that I witness walking that fine line of living in some abstract reality.

I mean, there is this white guy, with long hair. He always dresses in black leather pants and a long storm trooper coat and one of those leather hats. He wears this outfit no matter how hot it is outside. Every now and then I see him waiting for the bus with a cigar in his mouth. He's obviously lost in some heavy mental fantasy. But, he ain't hurtin' no one so I say, *"Rock on!"*

There's this other man… He's of Korean descent. I'm not quite sure of his story but he appears to be very normal—a least via his outward appearance. His clothes are always clean and his hair is combed. I see him walking around the neighborhood sometimes. Whenever he needs a smoke, he just crouches down and lights one up. Crouching there, in that position so commonly seen in Korea. My knees are so shot from my years in the martial arts that I could never sit there like that for more than a second or two. But, there he crouches, smoking his smoke as the cars pass by.

He walked in front of me in the self-serve checkout line at the supermarket once. They had just changed the store around. He was saying, *"Water, water?"* I guess he used to know where to get it but since the change-up he was lost. The store clerk tried to help him but to no avail. He just kept saying, *"Water, water?"* I don't know what eventually happened. But, he did not understand the instruction.

There's also this other Asian guy who roams my neighborhood. He is way more disheveled. He looks homeless but he obviously is not. This guy commonly whips out his dick. Sometimes I'll be driving by and there he will be playing with his tool. A couple weeks back I went to the gas station. There he was staring at a lady who was filling up. Out runs the owner of the station, *"Get out of here! Get out of here!"* I mean he was really yelling. I guess he was trying to protect his customers. He didn't want the guy to pull out his Johnson.

You know, there are a lot of people who walk a fine line of difference and exist in society. I mean, it wasn't that many years ago when people like I, who choose to grow their hair long, were total ostracized and thought to be of some mental defect. It's hard to imagine that today but I lived through it. People would yell stuff at us as we walked down the street. ...We wouldn't be served in restaurants. From this, we came to refer to ourselves as, *"Freaks."* It was a means to turn things around on the ones who were trying to define us as something wrong. But, were we? Or, were we simply different? ...Seeking a different definition of life and society and expressing it via our hair and our clothing.

Today, I saw this Asian lady sitting in the middle of the sidewalk. She had a bag from a local drug store in front of her and she was playing around with the stuff that was inside of it. She had this big smile on her face. I believe she was Korean. Was there anything wrong with this behavior—sitting there in the middle of the sidewalk? No. She wasn't bothering anyone and she seemed very happy doing what she was doing.

You know, some would say that I would not be the person I am today without the influence of Korean culture—via the martial arts, my marriage, my extended family, etc. And, they would be right. From that interaction, (and others), I have come to appreciate the fact that some people, especially those who are newly arrived into a new country, simply approach life in a manner that is somewhat different from the norm. They're not bad. What they are doing is not wrong. It is simply different. They are just doing what they have learned how to do in the way they have learned how to do it.

I think this is something that we all really need to think about. ...Something that we all really need to take into consideration. People do things differently. Some people step beyond the realms of the norm but that, in and of itself, does not make them bad. They are just different.

Just like in the '60s and the early '70s, for those of us with long hair, there were those people that wanted to cast judgement onto others no matter what. But, in doing so, they were illustrating their own limited level of human perception. They just wanted everyone to be they way they wanted them to be. They just wanted everyone to live their life the way they lived their own life. But, we're all different. We all have our own upbringings. We all have our own understandings. And, as long as what someone else is doing hurts no one else, why can't they be allowed to live what they live the way they want to live it without the harsh judgement of others?

So, next time you are about to cast your judgment onto someone, think about this… Ask yourself the question, *"What makes what I think and the way I do things right and what makes what someone else thinks and is doing wrong?"* Perhaps you will have a realization and realize that everyone should be allowed to be who and what they choose to make themselves to be.

As for the lady sitting there smiling while she played with the contents of her bag, good for her! A smile always makes everyone it encounters happier.

Next time you are thinking about judging someone, why don't you smile instead. That smile may make everyone's everything just a little bit better.

* * *
21/Dec/2021 08:20 AM

It is very easy to take.

It is very easy to consume.

What did you do yesterday to give?

What did you do yesterday to give something to someone who you care about or someone who has inspired you?

What are you going to do today?

Life is full of people making excuses. But, if you do not do something positive, if you do not give to those who have helped you, nothing is ever done.

Just Something Else to Take Your Mind Off of What's Really Important
20/Dec/2021 09:24 AM

I have been hearing all of this debate lately about whether or not *Die Hard* is a Christmas movie or not on all of the talking head TV shows and on the radio. Really... Who cares?

I remember when *Die Hard* first came out. I saw it on the Friday it was released at a local theater. This theater had a smaller screen and the sound system wasn't that great. The movie, however, was great. Immediately after the movie was completed I drove up to Westwood to see it again on the big screen. I thought it was that good.

Is it a Christmas movie? Well yes, it does take place surrounding the Christmas holiday. But again, who cares? That is not what the movie is about.

Here's the thing about life... Everybody, whether knowingly or not, tries to fill your mind with all kinds of bullshit so you will not think about the what is really important.

Think about your own life. What do you think about? Do you fill your thinking time with thoughts about the what really matters—about making your life and All Life better; doing something that is better for all? Or, do you drift to the meaningless? The current fantasy? Your current fantasy?

Turn on any TV, listen to the radio, watch YouTube, listen to the podcasters, they are all filled with a bunch of meaningless nothing all designed to take your mind away from what is truly important. They feed you some addictive substance—something that you will share with someone else. ...All designed to cause you to not look deeply into your life, your life actions, and how what you do not only affects you but the everyone else.

So, what are you going to do next? Think about the meaningless nothing someone has feed you? Or, choose to make your thoughts mean something—make them guide you to a better you—make them lead you to a better <u>all</u> for you and for everyone else?

What will be your next thought? Make that your meditation for the day.

What are you thinking about and why are you thinking it? Who or what guided you to thinking that thought? What will that thought do for your life? What will it do for or to the life of anyone else?

What will be your next thought and why will you be thinking it? Your life. Your choice.

*   *   *
20/Dec/2021 09:23 AM

The people with no true power always attempt to use whatever power they have to take over and dominate the life of someone else.

Toad Warrior VHS
18/Dec/2021 02:25 PM

It's interesting… Every now and then people hit me up on Facebook or Instagram or somewhere and tell me about the what's what of the what's going on.

Today, some guy contacted me, letting me know that an apparent Screener Copy of *Toad Warrior* was up for auction on eBay and he was wondering if he should bid on it.

I found all of this karmically serendipitous as I had, just the other day, written a blog mentioning *Max Hell Frog Warrior* AKA *Toad Warrior*.

Anyway, I took a look at the auction and I don't where the seller got that video tape but it was not an actual Screening Copy, at least not from the source: namely Don or I, even though it did have my name on it: Scott Shaw, *Toad Warrior*, Screener Copy, and a phone number. It must have been some sort of bootleg or something???

Here's a secret that you may not know and a way to tell if a VHS tape is an original or a fake for those of you who weren't in the film game back in the days of video tape. If there is video picture separation and a light glitching along one of the sides of the tape, normally the left side, it was a VHS-to-VHS transfer and not a transfer from a Beta Master. FYI.

More interesting than even that was/is the fact and the question, *"Why do these video tapes sell for so much money?"* I mean, I should sell the ones I have. They would equal a big chunk of change. Plus, they aren't a bootleg. They are a Valid Original. Even more than that, I could print more copies—make more money. I'm the one with the Masters collecting dust in my Film Vault. But, I was never about the money… I was just about the art… Stupid me…

Anyway, back to the question, what makes these video tapes so valuable? The quality of the picture and the sound are not that great. I mean, sure they take you back to a place in time but was a bad picture with not great sound actually a better viewing experience? I mean, the DVD is still available and you can watch *Toad Warrior* on Amazon Prime Video. So???

And remember, Don and I never wanted that version of the film to be released in the U.S. We didn't like the cut. I was forced to release it on DVD because someone/somehow, probably stolen from one of the screening houses, got a Beta copy of the film and then sold it to a distribution company who released it without our permission. Just a bit of history for you… Plus, if you truly care about the legacy of Donald G. Jackson, *Zen Filmmaking*, and myself you wouldn't try to make a buck by selling a bootleg copy of *Toad Warrior* on eBay.

In closing, this is just a note to all you people out there… Be warned… There's a lot of fakes. Maybe you don't care? I don't know? But, to whomever paid all that money for that video tape, just know that it is not a True Source Copy.

As for the guy who contacted me, I'm going to sent him one of the original video tapes of Toad Warrior; signed. A real Screening Copy. No charge.

Like I used to sign my letters back in the days of *Max Hell:*

This is Life.
This is Zen.
This is Scott Shaw Signing Out.
Zen Filmmaking!

*   *   *

18/Dec/2021 09:33 AM

What do you do everyday?

What are you addicted to?

If you can't control the small things that you do why do you believe you will be able to control the larger elements of your life?

Did You Get the Help that You Need?
18/Dec/2021 08:35 AM

Ever since the birth of the #metoo movement and the later #cancelculture movement I have watched and occasionally written about, here in this blog, how accusations have now become enough to take down a person's life. Just this week it happened again with that one actor.

As I've said before, I am not defending these people. If they've done something wrong and hurt someone, they've done something wrong and hurt someone and that's not right. But, why do the people proclaiming these proclamation do what they do so deep into time and why do they do them, *"Now,"* whenever that now may be? They all seem motivated by something. But, what?

Some of these accused people had the power to push through and maintain their life and their career. Others have not. But, does destroying someone livelihood and life correct any accused wrongs that they may have done? Does it change anything? And why were these charges not made then instead of now? It all leaves a lot of questions.

Interestingly, a few people have even tried to #cancel me online. People I never met and do not know. This all mostly happened before this stage of life-existence has come into play, however. Though I have not been accused of sexual deviance or anything like that, that's just not who I am, some have attacked my credibility and my artistic motivations. Of course, what they said was not true and simply a redefining of my life and my motivations in their own mind. Like Popeye says, *"I yam what I yam and that's all I yam."* But, more than all that, why attack someone like me? Why target me? Sure, I've made mistakes. We all have. But, I mean, my whole life has been about trying to help and make the All and the Everything just a little better in whatever small way I can. So???

Now, this piece is not about me. I'm just using myself as an example as it illustrates how anyone can say anything, be it truthful or not, in this era and lives are hurt. But, then what becomes the karma to the person doing the doing?

I watched this interesting documentary on Showtime a couple of weeks ago when it first came out, *Ricky Powell The Individualist*. It was about the The Rickister, as he was known, who was this photographer who was at the heart of the New York Rap and Street Culture scene when it was first rising in the early 1980s. He became one of those great snapshot photographers who really captured a lot of important history but ended up going down a dark road of crack addiction and a disheveled lifestyle eventually dying at the age of fifty-nine. Good doc! Check it out.

One of the most interesting elements of the doc that I found—something that really sent me to thinking, was that fact that he grew up with a single mother that was really into the then club culture. She would even take him along with her and stick him in a corner when he was a child. It really caused me to realize and to re-think about how many young people, myself included, who grew up with a single mother, (my father died when I was ten), were really guided down a pathway where there was no way that we were going to come out normal and psychologically sound. Add into this any physical and/or psychological abuse, (by its many definitions), and what was born was a child turning into a adult with this altered skillset and modified life understanding that drove some to do not good things. I mean, I have known so many people who grew up like me, with a single mother, and not one of them did not spend at least a certain portion of their life doing some bad (not good) stuff. Or, at least, spending a lot of time on a shrink's couch.

Now, this ditty is not only about people who grew up with single mothers who messed with their minds. It's about anyone who grew up in a situation that caused them to emerge into adulthood with a less than ideal frame of psychological and life behavior reference.

The question then arises, *"Did you get the help that you need?"* I mean, there is help out there. But, getting it—going to get it, is never easy. It's not easy to find. It's not easy to admit to yourself that you need help. Most who need it, live in denial. It's never easy to force yourself to take that first step and that second step.

I think this is where one of the biggest problems of life is born. Particularly with the people who do bad things…

…And, if I can sidebar here: It's not just the people who are accused of doing bad things but also the people doing the accusing because that is, or at least may be, a bad deed, as well…

But, back to the people: At least most people were not born with some mental defect. They were life-programmed into their patterns of behavior. And, for many/most this occurred when they were young.

Now obviously, some people rise to a position of power and from that they allow that power and their ability to dominate others to take control of their mind and set a negative pattern of behavior into motion. They do bad and power-tripping things to others. Not good! This happens in life and this certainly happens on the internet. We've all seen it. But, what is the root cause of that behavior? Where was that mindset born? Where did someone come to think that it was okay to do something like that? Most likely, it was born in their childhood and how they were raised.

How were you raised? Did you have a good childhood? If you did, how has that taught you to behave towards others? Did you have a bad or disturbed childhood, (however you want to define that)? If you did, how has that taught you to behave towards others?

Most people never take the time to study these questions. Most people never take the time to study themselves. They just do what they do with excuses a plenty

...If they make any excuses at all. Some just do. They feel right in their actions. How about you? How do you behave and why? How do you treat others and why?

For the people who do study themselves, they may find that they need help. Do they reach out for it is the question? Do they find it? How about you?

Let's get back to the source of all this... What do you do that hurts the life of someone else? No matter what your reasoning and/or your why; why do you do it? Do you feel justified in your actions simply because you can do it? Do you ever study, care, or even think about the ramifications of your actions? If you don't—if you hope to hurt someone else, no matter what your logic, how does that describe who and what you actually are? Step back from yourself; what kind of person would do that? Would you want it done to you?

I think back to this statement the actress Camryn Manheim made to an interviewer on TV early in the launch of the #metoo movement. She said, *"If I went to a hotel room with a man, I knew why I was going there."* What she illustrates in that statement is someone taking responsibility for their actions. How many people do that? Particularly in this age of the internet where anyone can say anything?

But ultimately, what all life comes down to is you. You are the one who creates your life situations. You are the one who will have to eventually pay the consequences. Whether you find yourself on the receiving end or the instigating end, there will always be a price to pay. Plus, it is far easier to cast the blame onto someone else than to personally take responsibly for what occurred to you due to your own level of choice and due to your own responsibility in any life situation. Casting blame is simply an excuse. It is a person's way to never share in any blame.

This is why knowing you—finding you, learning to be the best you that you can be is essential. Many of us had a hard childhood that left us scared. ...That left us doing less than ideal things. But, there is help. Are you willing to find it and get it? Are you willing to stop yourself or learn how to stop yourself from doing things that hurt you or hurt anyone else for any reason? Are you willing to take the responsibility for fixing what you've broken—helping those who you've hurt? Or, are you just lost in your own Self-Rightness? If you are, you should really think about who and what you are and the wake you are leaving.

Many people in this era feel it is their right to attack. But, attack only equals counterattack. From your attack or your counterattack, you may emerge the winner but then what? What comes next? Did it make you a better person? Does it make your adversary a lessor person? And, whose going to pay the karma; as there is always karma?

The ultimate truth of life is, there is no one to blame but you. You did what you did. You can blame someone else all you want but no one but you feels what you feel; no one but you did what you did. No one but you has the power to control the true inner you.

So, what are you going to do next? Are you going to attack? Are you willing to suffer the karmic consequences of your actions? Then what? It goes on and on and on. Or, you can just be good. Say good things. Do good things. Fix what you've broken when you can. Forgive those who hurt you and move on. Help everyone. And, understand that we are created in our childhood. Some of us had less than ideal examples of how to live our life. Some of us where taught the wrong way to encounter and treat others. But, it's only you who can fix any of that. Will you? Will you fix you and stop seeking to blame and to hurt the life or someone/anyone else?

Alone Together
17/Dec/2021 07:49 AM

Maybe you are laying down sleeping next to someone. You are having this elaborate, very involved dream. It is all going on in your mind. You know it is happening but the person sleeping next to you has no idea what is going on in your brain.

Maybe you are on an airplane. You have fallen asleep and you are dreaming whatever it is you are dreaming. The stewardess comes to wake you up to serve you your breakfast. She has no idea of all the images, the words spoken, and the dream-life that was being lived in your mind.

Maybe you are sitting back. There is this vast fantasy going on in your mind. You are seeing it lived in your mind's eye but that is the only place it is being lived. The person or the persons who make up that fantasy have no idea of what you and only you are envisioning in your psyche. Though you have dragged them into your fantasy, your fantasy is not their fantasy. They may not even know who you are and/or may never even think of you if they do know who you are.

How much of your life is lived only in your mind? For each of us, we live this vast second life in our dreams. A life that we have no control over. While dreaming, we encounter this vast experience that may or may not be linked to our real life but it is enacted in some abstract plane of reality that is only known by our own individual mind.

For each of us, we live at least a certain portion of our life cast to the realms of fantasy. We may envision all of the actions and fantasy-life interactions lived with other people that have no idea they were dragged into our mind's eye of fantasy.

Some refute this style of life living as it is believed to contribute nothing to the truth of true reality. Others, as it is all they have—as their true life is unfulfilled, spend many a life hour lost in this realm of untruth. But, is it actually untruth or it is simply life not lived in the human form?

You are alone. That is the ultimate truth of reality. Though you may have one or a million people that believe they care about you, in the end, all you feel, all you experience, the you that is the true you, is only you. No one can feel what you feel. No one else can live what you live. Ultimately, you are alone.

In your alone, we each live a second life that is lost only to our own mind.

When you are gone what becomes of all the life you lived in your dreams and in your fantasies? As these moments were not lived on the physical plane of reality, where what you do actually equals something, what did all of those moments lost only to your mind actually mean?

You can live in your mind if you want to. In sleep, in dreams, we really have no choice.

You can live in your mind if you want to. But, fantasy equals nothing more than the ultimate self-ingested drug of illusion.

So, what are you going to live with your life? What will be your legacy? True reality? A reality that is lived on the physical plane of accepted actuality—a place where what you do actually changes the course of your life and the direction of the life of other people? Or, a space lost only to your own mind where nothing actually means anything—nothing more than a flash projection of a life never actually lived?

Anybody Want to Make Another Frogtown Movie?
16/Dec/2021 12:43 PM

You know, having been in this film game for a long-long time now, I have encountered and experienced so many things. I've met and worked with some really great people and I've met and worked with some real assholes. The thing about Hollywood, and I'm putting, *"Hollywood,"* in Air Quotations is that here, the people are after something; they want to achieve something. Many/most hope to be stars in however they envision that delineation. The one thing for sure is, they definitely want something and they are willing to work for it and work towards it.

Then, there is the everyone else. The everyone out there who simply wants to throw stones but creates no true film projects of their own. I mean, you don't have to be in Hollywood to create great cinema. You can do great cinema anywhere. There have been so many great projects that came from the Out There. The Any Where.

I think that's why critics should really prove their worth, in the realms of cinema, before they step up to the pulpit and criticize others. 'Cause if you ain't made a movie, you ain't made a movie. And, if the filmmaker you are critiquing can't return the favor, that's pretty disingenuous don't you think?

All this being said, I make movies all the time. In these later years I've focused much more on visual cinema and have left the story telling behind. That just seemed like a natural progression for me. This is not to say that I don't miss the camaraderie and the human interaction that comes from creating story-driven cinema.

Sadly, times have changed in the world of Indie Cinema. Once upon a time everyone was happy to jump in and help. Give them an acting role and they were happy to show up. Give them the crew position they wanted and desired to build their resume upon and they were there. It wasn't always perfect. But, most people were true and honest about their desires and motivations and they were willing to give and to help. Then it became hard to trust anyone. Even on the No Budget Indie level you had to get things like production insurance and all that as you never knew what snake may be hiding in the bush that would come out and sue you. I don't know… Things just changed…

Certainly, in my years of creating cinema, I have had some great people who stepped up to the plate to help. Aside from Don Jackson, there were friends like Julie Strain, Kevin Eastman, Kenneth H. Kim, Rich Magram, and Kevin Thompson. Each provided a great service to a finished film or films.

As a filmmaker, I have experienced, and as I just alluded to a moment ago, there are those out there who do nothing but criticize. I always found that very shallow as we all have our options but to try to frame a person's creative project defined by your own mindset and your own predetermined expectations seems fairly shallow, don't you think?

One of my films which has experienced a lot of critique, both in terms of the negative and the positive is, *Max Hell Frog Warrior*. The responses have always amused me as people have tried to find some deep meaning and/or simply a reason to find fault where there really is none. It's a Zen Film people! It's *Zen Filmmaking!* There is no story! There is no point or purpose! Like Zen, it just is! Plus, it only cost like a hundred dollars to make. Yet, this has never stopped the naysayers. And, that's okay. If talking negatively about a film or a filmmaker makes you feel some kind of way, that's your business. But, you should really think about the karma in all that.

Several years back now, this film school student hit me up and did an extensive interview with me on the film. *Max Hell Frog Warrior: The Facts and the Fiction* was the title of the piece. You can find a copy of it on this website if you look and in a few other places. Good piece! The guy really thought out his questions. And, the fact is, twenty years deep into the release of that film, that guy was the first journalist to actually interview me about that movie. Pretty crazy; right? All those reviewers talk about it, but nobody asked me (or Don) until that point in time.

I started to do a sequel a number of years ago. I was planning to title it: *Max Hell Verses the Lizard People*. But, some crazy shit was going and I never finished it. Time has gone by and I just think I'm going to let that footage go. Maybe after I'm dead, someone will put it together.

All this being said, like I said, once upon a time people who wanted to be an actor, an actress, or participate in the creation of a film, brought something to the table. More than just themselves and the promise that they (someday) were going to be a star, they provided locations, equipment, make-up services, other actors, other crew members, something... They didn't just show up full of ego, expecting to be paid handsomely and to be treated like a star.

This morning, I was digging for something in the back of my closet and I found a couple of age-old frog masks I have. You know, one of those things you forget about until it is in front of your face. It made me think maybe I should do another Frogtown movie. I mean, people are always contacting me about the film, asking about the Rights because they want to do a comic book but pay me nothing. No!

I don't know, it may be fun...

And, *Max Hell* is just an idea based on rediscovering those frog masks. It could be RB7 based. *Samurai Vampire* based. Or, something entirely new. I've got tons and tons of ideas. But, I think outside participation would be the key for me to get back into the story-driven game. So, I don't know??? Maybe??? What do you think? Anybody want to make another Frogtown movie?

* * *
15/Dec/2021 01:09 PM

What will happen when the memory of you is forgotten?

Someone Else's Money
14/Dec/2021 12:51 PM

So… How is it that you come by your money? How is it that you get the money to buy the things that you need? How is it that you get the money to buy the things that you want?

Most people never think about any of this. They just do whatever it is they do to get their money.

The problem is, if you don't think about how you come by getting your money you can create an entire world of bad effects not only for you but for other people and possibly the entire world.

Again, how do you come by your money? What do you do to get your money? Take a moment and really chart this out.

Most people justify whatever it is they are doing as long as they get the money they need. They really don't care what their doing is doing to anyone or anything else, nor do they understand what their doing is doing to themselves. How about you? How does what you do to get your money affect yourself; anyone or everyone else? Truly, ask yourself this question and come up with a truthful answer.

Some people believe that as long as what they are doing is legal, what they are doing to get paid is just fine. But, is it? What karma is attached to what you do to get money.

Getting paid has changed a lot since the dawning of the internet. And, it has continued to evolve. Though some people do the same jobs that have been done for generations to make their money, other people do different things today than what was done even a few years ago. So again, clearly detail what it is you do to make your money. What does it mean to you and your life, what does it mean to that anyone else, and what does it mean to that person who pays you?

Most people make their money via other people paying them for doing something that they do. In some cases, this is a traditional job: physical or mental labor equaling a something. Some own personal businesses that creates the interplay of having to please your customers or there will be no business. Others, get paid via nefarious means. They knowing do things that will hurt someone or something else to get their money. Not good but that is reality. Still others do very abstract things like create art or critique the art others have created. Whatever the case, the money someone pays you to do something causes you to enter into the realms of an interpersonal relationship with that person or persons and this is where many of the problems with life and with karma begin.

Think about the people who pay you for doing what you do. What do you owe them and why? Again, most people never think about any of this. But, the moment someone pays you, you owe them something. The problem with this, *"Something,"* is, that something is different in the mind of each person.

Most people simply skim over this fact in life. They just think about the money they are making. They don't think what taking the money from someone else actually means.

What does it mean? Are you completely oblivious to the fact that the moment someone pays you, you owe them. The what you owe them is the only question.

When some people do not do what they are paid for, they are fired. For others, they are chastised. Yet, for others what occurs becomes much more villainous. We've all heard stories. But, the fact of the fact is, if the person seeking to get paid did not place themselves in a position of servitude in the first place to that other individual nothing negative could have ever occurred.

Think how many people dislike the people who pay or give them money. Think how many people hate their bosses. Think how many people dislike the people who they must do whatever it is they do to get paid. Even the people who own businesses, and get paid by clientele, own that person giving them money their entire life as all that they own is provided by them. But, how many people think about this?

Here is the ultimate truth to all of this, if you take money from someone/anyone, you own that person everything, because they are the one keeping you alive.

So, here's the thing, and you can lie to yourself all you want, but it does not change the truth; if you receive money from anyone for any reason you owe that person everything because they are the one who is providing you with a means to survive.

Think about it... And, once you do think about it, take a long hard look at your life and decide who you owe what to and why. How did you make your money to survive? And, how can you pay back all of those people who provided you with the money to live your life as you have and own the things that you own?

You can take by whatever means you want to claim your deservedness but from every person you take you owe that person everything. So, who do you owe? How are you going to pay them back for providing you with a life?

*   *   *
14/Dec/2021 08:08 AM

If you study the evolution of your life and if you are honest with yourself you will find that most of the things that have happened to you, both positive and negative, were your fault.

* * *

13/Dec/2021 09:30 AM

It's easy to tell someone what they are doing is wrong.

It is much hard to actually do something right yourself.

* * *

13/Dec/2021 08:55 AM

Say you get your revenge on someone. That means that you hurt someone or did something negative to them.

Doesn't that cause them to seek revenge on you? Then what?

When a Cult Isn't a Cult
13/Dec/2021 08:23 AM

  I watched *Tiger King III* over the weekend. In this segment of the now on-going series they focused on a Tiger-guy whose Sanskrit name was Bhagavan. He was a claimed disciple of my spiritual teacher, Swami Satchidananda. Now, I never met this man. It appears that he came into the fold later that I was there. He also was on the East Coast where I was a West Coast kid.
  The thing that I found somewhat surprising about this series is that in the first two episodes of the three-part series they really forced a lot on Swami Satchidananda. They continually bad-mouthed the man and they continually said that he lead was a cult leader, which helped to form the mindset of the Tiger-guy Bhagavan.
  You know, whenever someone doesn't understand something they call it a, *"Cult."* Whenever something is different from the norm, they call it a, *"Cult."* Whenever something is new and exploratory, they call it a, *"Cult."* I was at the heart of the Integral Yoga Institute, I was a direct student of Swami Satchidananda, and I can tell you, and I've said all of this before, it was not a, *"Cult!"*
  The people who lived at the Integral Yoga Institute, who were not monks, all had jobs. They had to pay rent. Even some of the Swami's had jobs. No one ever told anyone how to dress, as was implied in *Tiger King III*. You could wear anything that you wanted. Yes, things like vegetarianism were suggested. Yes, it was suggested that you don't do drugs and don't drink alcohol, as it is not good for you. It was taught not to smoke as it is bad for you and everyone else. Yes, if someone wanted to learn how to do the physical aspects of yoga or learn how to meditate, this was the place to go. But, people could eat or drink or do anything that they wanted as long as they didn't do it on the property. No one was recruited. No one was ever asked to

stay. There were no people out there trying to find new disciples. There was nothing like that. It was simply a place and a teaching that offer people a way to live a healthier and more spiritual way of life based in the East Indian tradition, if that is what they wanted.

I mean, think about it. Isn't the Christian Church a cult? Isn't the Islamic faith a cult? Isn't the Jewish faith a cult? All of these traditions suggest to people what they should or should not do. They all tell people what they believe is right and wrong. What they are teaching is simply more established in the minds of the masses. In India, what Swami Satchidananda taught is simply the understood, expected norm. There, his teachings were long established throughout history. In India he was not a cult leader, he was simply a teacher—one of many.

Was Swami Satchidananda the perfect man? No. I've spoken and I've written about all of this before. Did some people idolize him? Yes. But, that is just the way some people are—that is how life is. Some people idolize movies stars, music stars, or sports stars. In this case, some people idolized a yogi. Was that asked for or required? Absolutely not. I never idolized him.

Now, I've detailed my time with this man and his organization in many places. Swami Satchidananda and his Integral Yoga Institute and the Sufi Order (under the guidance of Pir Vilayat Khan), were essential parts to my early years in life. I was an initiate of both and I, at least hope, I provided a worthy service and good example to both of these organizations. I was Swami Satchidananda's West Coast sound man. Though I was young I had a skill-set that was needed and could be used. As for the Sufi Order, I helped them at the Renaissance Faire booth each year. I was asked to the be guy that collected the $2.00 entry fee for people to attended the Tuesday night Sufi Dances (the Dances of Universal Peace). Though I did not like doing that job, as I always felt they should be free. I mean, in all of the years I taught the marital arts, I did it for free. But, I understood the need for the exchange of money and I helped in the way that I could.

All this being said, yes both of these pathways and teachings were different from the Westernized understanding of the norm. But, was anything bad going on? No, absolutely not. Were they a cult? No.

And, I've talked about this before, as well... When I decided it was time for me to leave, I was gone. Nobody tried to hold me back. My life moved onto other places. Yes, Swami Satchidananda and the Sufi Order are still in my heart. Yes, I learned a lot from both of them. Yes, I would not be the person I am today without my interaction with them. But, were they a cult? No.

I believe that one of the problems with the world is, wherever someone feels that someone else has done something wrong they attempt to concoct a reason why. They try to find a focus of blame. But, the fact is, some people just do fucked up things. Some people are not good people. Some people go to a teacher like Swami Satchidananda and take away the good. Others look for a reason to find the bad.

But, good or bad is all a point of view. If you love Hell it becomes Heaven. Yes, there are people that do some very messed up things with their life. But, what and/or who defines that wrongness? Should it be you? Are you without sin? Is it the documentarians who are looking for people who will say bad things about Swami Satchidananda? Are they without sin?

I am not supporting or standing up for and/or undermining anyone's hurt. If you were hurt you were hurt. But, to try to blame another man for what someone else, (male or female), does is not the true path to righteousness. It is simply a person looking for a justifiable excuse and a reason why when there truly are none. People are who they. People do what they do. If anyone is casting the shadow of blame onto anyone, that is the person who should be studied as they are the one with something to hide.

* * *

12/Dec/2021 07:14 AM

If you receive a gift that you don't want, is it a gift at all?

If you give a gift that they don't want, is it a gift at all?

Is a Master Truly a Master?
10/Dec/2021 10:54 AM

I want to talk a little bit about the evolution and the practical development of the modern martial arts, particular focused on their development here in the U.S. This may be a bit obscure for you readers out there, not involved with the martial arts, but hopefully you may gain some general life understanding from what I write.

First of all, at the outset of their piece, it must be understood that the modern martial arts have become a very egocentric system of human development. People are very-very focused and orientated on their style, their school, and their teacher. From this is born an enormous amount of criticism directed at other practitioners, other styles, other instructors, and other associations. In fact, from my experience, some of the martial artists I have encountered have been the most petty people I have ever interacted with in my life. It's sad really. And, the truth be told, all any martial artists out there reading this has to do is to look at their own thoughts, their own words, their own behavior, and the words and the behavior of those other martial artists they know or have encountered to confirm this fact.

This has always really bother me. Even when I was a child and adolescent practitioner, it really distressed me that other martial artists would so vehemently go after practitioners from other traditions and schools. Even within specific schools, students would go after other students. But, how does this style of behavior help to make anything any better?

I remember when I was about twenty-one, I was asked to help judge a promotion test at the school of this one, then very famous, Korean-born Taekwondo instructor. The man himself was a very good practitioner. One of those guys with just beautiful kicks. Anyway, one of his students, testing for a blue belt, did not do very well in the kicking segment of the test. You know, some people just do not have the potential to be a great kicker due to their body design and things like that. The instructor just ripped into him, really putting him down. It had to be very embarrassing for the man as there were a lot of spectators in attendance. My thought at the time was, *"You're his instructor. Isn't his technical ability, or lack thereof, at least partially your fault?"*

Later on, during that evening of testing, an old-school Korean, *"Master,"* gave a small demonstration. The man, obviously older, was just not technically very good. But, did this young instructor rip into him? No. So, you see there's all this interplay of personality and projected desires in the martial arts even within a specific school. I just never believed that the martial arts was the place for this style of behavior.

One of the other interesting, and very illustrative of an era, things that took place during this same time period was that there was this one, also very well-known, Korean-born Taekwondo instructor, here in the L.A. area. This was during the time when the names and the rank on Korean certificates were handwritten. His black belt certificate, which hung on the wall of his studio, looked to show that he was a 7th dan black belt. But, if you could read Korean, you would see that his rank number in Korean was one. Making him a 1st dan black belt. He had simply added a line to the top of the one, on the English portion of the certificate, making it into a seven.

Another interesting illustration is that I think back to when I was in my final year of college, earning my B.A. in Geography from California States University, Northridge. One of my required courses was this group project class. For us, we were doing a spatial analysis and demographic study on the then up-and-coming community of Palmdale, California. Each Saturday we would drive out to Palmdale and do our required part of the study. At one point, I was walking through the old downtown section of the city and I saw this martial art studio. By this point in my life I was operating my own studio so I was obviously drawn to the place. I look in the window and this school owner had his certificates clearly displayed. He was a seventh-degree black belt of Taekwondo, a seventh-degree black belt of some brand of Karate, a seventh-degree black belt of some style of Kung Fu, and he held high ranks in a couple of other systems of self-defense, as well. The certificates we all issued by the same organization that I had never heard of. Anyone who understands anything about the martial arts will know, that yes, an advanced practitioner could readily learn the techniques and the forms of another system. But, to hold such advanced legitimate ranks in all of these highly differing system of self-defense is simply impossible. The point being, this style of deception has been going on for a very long time. People bought into it then and they buy into it now.

As a journalist, I have been asked to write articles about so many schools and practitioner's business methods that it is not even funny. I can't even remember how many articles I have written. Most of the people I spoke with are nice. Some are just flat-out liars. But, more than a couple of the school owners would discuss the fact that they had students who when they rose to level of the black belt would leave their teacher, open their own school, and siphon many of their previous instructor's students away from the school by bad mouthing their teacher. I mean, if where you learned all that you learned was from that man (or woman) how can you criticize them? But, that's what is done.

For better of for worse, I was alive, a part of, and a witness to, the birth of the modern Korean marital arts here in America. I was there and present when the first wave of Korean marital arts instructors arrived from Korea. Back then, simply because a person was of Asian descent, they received preferential respect simply because they were who they were. Some of these newly arrived instructors were very-very good practitioners and nice people. Many, however, were not. Even myself, I got taken advantage of and, in fact, cheated by some of these so called, *"Masters."* The stories I could tell…

The thing is, many marital art instructors, no matter how technically proficient they may be, see the martial arts simply as a business. From this, they do dishonorable things, make unscrupulous comments, and even lie about who and what they are. I personally know that a number of the first-generation instructors lied about where they learned what they learned and who they learned it from. You don't have to just listen to me, ask anyone else who was there and knows the truth about the history of the modern Korean martial arts. The fact is, now many of those first-generation masters are no longer with us. Thus, their truth, or the lack thereof, will never be known. Their fabrications died with them. But, why did they do any of this? It was all based on money, ego, and outward notoriety projection. And, this style of behavior is still going on.

Some, even famed founders, saw money as more important than the tradition of the art they laid claim to. They believed they were so technically advanced that they could teach a student in weeks or months what was understood to take years to have actually comprehended. With this ideology as a basis, they would rapidly award some of their so-called student advanced rank that took those who followed the traditional path years-upon-years to achieve. Thus, rank became the focal point of the martial arts in America, which led to an untold number of lies begin told and certificates being sold. Combine this with all of the bad mouthing that went on, and still goes on, and what are we left with? I don't even have an answer for that but it is not good.

What should be a true pathway to physical and mental enlightenment has been denigrated into an ego and money making machine. The fact is, it does not matter who is better at what. It doesn't matter who can do what technique better than someone else. It doesn't matter what insult and criticism one practitioners throws at someone else. It certainly doesn't matter what rank a person holds when ranks are bought and sold on the open market. What matters is that the martial arts should not be about criticism. The martial arts should not be about judgment. The martial arts should not be about ego. The martial arts should be about a pathway for the betterment of all.

I don't know how any of this can be corrected because all I see is a mess. Yes, there are some great technicians. Yes, there are some great teachers. But, more than not, mostly what is there is a lot of low-level human behavior and ego-driven individuals claiming, *"I am this, you are not."*

For you martial artists out there, how do you behave? Really think about this question. What do you say? What do you do? How do you refer to and/or discuss other practitioners, styles, schools, and organizations? As I say time-and-time again, all life begins with you. What have you said? What have you done? More importantly, what have you said to undo the negative things that you previously said? What have you done to undo the negative things that you previously have done? If you don't critique yourself first—if you don't tell the world your flaws first—if you don't right your own wrongs, what gives you the right to cast judgement onto someone else? If you are claiming to be a master but you base your life upon negativity, on any level, are you truly a master?

The martial arts should be a bastion of goodness and positive instruction. Is it? I don't know? I guess that is defined individually by each practitioner, each instructor, each school, and each organization. What I can say is, it all begins with you: what you say, what you do, and how you behave. So, (and not just for your martial artists out there), if you want to make anything better, be the source point for that betterment and stop all/any of the negativity. Turn off your ego. Turn off your criticism. Let all things be as they are. Then all life gets to exist in its natural state of perfection.

* * *

10/Dec/2021 09:37 AM

If your only contribution is critique and criticism that means that you have created nothing of your own.

No Pride in the Doing
09/Dec/2021 03:47 PM

How often do you do something for someone and don't tell them that you did it? How often do you do something for someone and expect nothing in return? How often do you do something for someone and take no pride in that fact that you did it?

When someone does something bad to someone it is most often then that they will say nothing. Yes, some very low-level people take pride in the fact that they say or do something to a person that affects their life in some negative manner. Most people aren't like that, however. They don't want to do things that hurt people.

What most people do want is to be acknowledge for what they have done. They want to be thanked. They want as many people as possible to be aware of the fact that they did something that made someone's something a little or a lot bit better. How about you?

Based in the Hindu understanding of life, there is Karma Yoga. What Karma Yoga witnesses is a person doing something good, positive, and/or helpful but then receiving no reward for their action(s). Though this all sounds great in concept, how many people behave like that? Even in spiritual circles when someone is doing that supposedly good and giving something, they will immediately state, *"I'm doing Karma Yoga."* That, in and of itself, kills the entire process.

So, here's the question for you, when was the last time you did something good or positive for someone and never said anything to anyone? The deed was just done and no one knew you did it. When was the last time you did something like that?

With all of this as a basis for thought, here's the assignment for the day (or everyday): Go and do something good for someone and tell no one you did it.

The thing is, you may feel no great sense of accomplishment—except maybe in your own mind. No one will thank you. This being said, the good thing you have done will make someone's life just a little bit better. What more of a reward do you need than that?

Try it. Observe the results. It may make you think a whole new way about life. It may make your giving that much more unencumbered by your desire for appreciation.

Give/do and tell no one. Watch how everybody's everything becomes just a little bit better.

Think About the Other Person First
08/Dec/2021 01:51 PM

It's not uncommon that I discuss the actions that I encounter when I am out driving. As stated many times, the way a person drives reveals what kind of person they truly are and how they will treat other life and this world as a whole.

In the news recently, they stated that even though we have been in the grips of the pandemic for over a year and a half now, 2021 was the worst year for highway fatalities in over a decade; at least here in California. I believe it. For a moment there, when the pandemic was in full swing and everything was shut down, you could drive the notoriously crowded L.A. freeways with no problem. But, that time is long gone. I have watched as people seemingly just no longer care that anyone else is on the road. I mean, people are driving crazy! Hell, just two months ago my car got totaled when this junky old Ford pickup sideswipe me. That guy got to go on with his life as he was driving a crappy old example of American steel. Me, he turned my life into a mess. But, did he/does he care? No. All he did was to think about was himself. He even lied to my insurance company. Thank god, I took photos of the accident so he didn't get away with it. But, that's sadly how some people behave. They care about no one but themselves.

It's easy to see this trait in people. Just watch how they talk to, talk about, and interact with others. But, that's not the point of this piece...

Today, I encountered an ideal example of what has become of drivers and how they think of no one else.

I went to the supermarket today to grab some salmon and veggies for dinner tonight. I bought the food, went back to my car, and started to pull out. I was about three quarters of the way out of the spot when this sedan jets by me nearly ripping into my rear bumper. If I didn't see them and stop, there would have been an accident. Okay… That's just how people have been driving lately. …Not giving a fuck about anyone else.

Anyway, I proceed toward the exit. There's this stop sign at the crossroads before you actually hit the supermarket's driveway out to the street. The car that swooped by me stops at that stop sign. What happened next, I almost couldn't believe. I see the driver's door open. I thought maybe the driven wanted to say, *"Sorry,"* to me or something like that or maybe just spit on the street like so many rude drivers do. But, the lady driver: middle aged, of Middle Eastern descent, gets out of her car and starts to walk towards the bank which was across the street. What! By this point, I'm not the only car behind her trying to leave the parking lot. I give a little honk just to let her know that there are cars trying to get out. She turns, looks at me, and continue to walk. I really couldn't believe it. She was using that stop sign as a parking spot.

Normally, I avoid confrontation. I've just seen so much of the bullshit that people unleash that I just let it go. But today, I roll down my window, *"Are you kidding me!"* She knew what she as doing. She just waved at me, like I was supposed to drive around her stop sign parked car. *"Think about the other person first,"* I exclaim.

You know, here we are, the real world… Most people don't behave like that woman. Most people try to be nice. Most people care about the other person. I know I do. I try to make everywhere I go just a little bit better. How about you? Do you zoom in behind people when they are backing out of their parking spot or do you let them pull out? Do you stop your car and park at a stop sign just because it will put you a little closer to where you want to be? This, even though you will totally hold up traffic.

You know, life is weird. People do weird things all the time. All you have to do is look around and you will see it.

I have definitely witnessed and observed that since the rebirth of driving culture emerged post the onslaught of the pandemic, drivers have changed. And, not for the better. But, that doesn't make it right. That doesn't make people doing rude, selfish, and uncaring things okay. But, like I say time and time again, all life begins with you. It begins with what you do. It begins by how you treat others.

How do you treat others? Do you consider them or do you only consider you? If you only consider you, is that the right way to live? And, if this/that is your modus operandi, what is your excuse for behaving like that?

I'm sure the lady today, had/has no excuse. She just doesn't give a fuck about anyone else. But, if you hurt the life of one person, you have hurt the entire world. Then, don't complain when bad shit comes your direction. Because you are the one who set it all in motion.

You know, when the cars stopped coming the other direction, I drove out and around her and drove on. I looked in my rear view as I finally left the parking lot. Her car was still there, while others struggled to get around her. Welcome to life.

So… All I can say is, think about the other person first. Really, it will make your, theirs, and everybody's everything just that much better.

Late into the Late Night
08/Dec/2021 07:26 AM

    I woke up after having fallen asleep watching the movie, *Jackie Brown*. I'm sure this is an AGAIN situation, as it is one of those great pieces of cinema that they play time-after-time-after-time on the late-night networks. And, as I tend to stay up way to late, it is not uncommon that I fall asleep in front of the TV, waking up with my legs in pain and a body that hurts. Trust me when I tell you, there is a high price to pay if you have lived a life defined by the martial arts.

    Anyway, Pam Grier was always one of my deep creative fantasies. Beautiful and a great actress—coming up in the time that I did and doing all of those great Blaxploitation, and otherwise, cinema epics. I always wished I could create a film with her. And, I wished that long before Jackie Brown. In fact, I wished I could work with so many other great actors and actresses from that era. I did get to work with Don Stroud and Karen Black. What GREAT actors and people! Now, so many of that era are gone—so many of the people I wished I could have worked with have left their life behind. I often wonder if I were to be offered a gig where I had the kind of money to pay the people I would truly want to work with, who would I call-up as so many of the Greats are gone. Think of even the *Zen Filmmaking* Crew, so many of them are now gone; Julie Strain and William Smith just this year. Like the Buddhist chant goes, *Gate, Gate, Paragate, Parasom Gate, Bodhi Swahi.* Gone, gone, gone to the other shore beyond, gone to the great awakening.

    But, back to the late night... I'm one of those people who pays way too much to get all of those Out There networks, that show oh so many movies that you (meaning I) don't really want to watch. I have millions of movies and shows offered to me and yet I find it so hard to find something worth watching. Movies, or pieces thereof, I've just seen way too many times… Movies like Black Hawk Down, (one of the best orchestrated movies ever), I still don't know how they achieved that, *Casino, Scarface, Boogie Nights, Saturday Night Fever, Road House,* and *Jackie Brown.* Movies like that; they're on all the time…

Speaking of *Road House*… I used to end up at auditions with his brother, Don Swayze all the time. I guess it was when they wanted that wayward looking White guy type. I imagine he got a lot more of those parts than I did, as he was who he was. Me, I eventually stopped going to additions. I mean, what was the point? If you want me for a film or a TV spot or a commercial, you can just let me know. Maybe I will take it, maybe I won't. But, all of those frantic drives across the city in a rush, hoping I will get there on time, through traffic and otherwise, just to take a shot at a dream that you (I) will never get—a possible dream being handed to you… …Dreams that will never come true. The stories I could tell you… It's just not worth it.

But again, here/there I was, waking up after falling asleep to a great film, late into the late night.

Maybe this is poetry, I don't know? Maybe this is inspiration for a dream, I don't know? Maybe this is simply being reminded of something I can never live? Maybe… It's all a big maybe? But, falling asleep and then waking up to a great piece of cinema, with your aging bones hurting… I don't know? Maybe it means something other than nothing. I will pretend that it does.

* * *
07/Dec/2021 09:08 AM

Who do you owe?

Why do you owe them?

What do you do owe them?

How much time and energy do you spend paying them back?

* * *

07/Dec/2021 07:47 AM

When you have five minutes left to live, wasting even a second becomes unthinkable.

How much of your life are you wasting?

Finding Enlightenment in the Mundane
AKA Meditation Does Not Have to Hurt
06/Dec/2021 03:40 PM

I have always believed that one must make the mundane their pathway to enlightenment. I mean, let's face facts, most of life is not all that exciting. It is not all that adrenalizing. Sure, there are those moments when great things happen and they make you feel really good—be those moments spiritually-based or otherwise. But, they are few and far between. Most of life is not like that.

The thing is, once certain people feel that heart pumping excitement, they constantly seek it out. This is true for worldly people and this is true for those walking the Spiritual Path, as well. Once they get hit with that first Satori or that initial Peak Experience, they know that kind of stuff exists and they try to find it again and again.

The thing about Spiritual Experience is, however, the moment you set it as your goal, your finding it becomes completely impossible. Because once it is that sought after something, it becomes that thing that can never be had—it is set somewhere off there in the unhaveable distance. Desired but never known.

This is the thing... People make spirituality a sought after something. They make it a goal. They are taught that they must sit and meditate for X amount of time or they are not a true practitioner. They are told, they must give up sex, they must give up all desire, they must shun all materialism, they must live a humble life, and reject all forms of ego. Sure, all this is great if that is who you are. But, most people are not like that. Most fight to meditate. Most beat themselves up over their desires. Many hate themselves for not being totally pure of thought. But, all this does is to set one into a constant state of turmoil. The fact is, thoughts and behavior like this remove one from true spirituality.

Meditation does not have to hurt! Being spiritual does not have to become a burdensome chore. It can be free. It can be natural. But, this is defined by how you approach it.

If you allow all of your life to be a spiritual progression, then you are living a truly spiritual life. You do not have to force yourself to do anything. You simply need to tune into that place in you which is naturally spiritual.

You can make anything your meditation. It does not have to be just you sitting there cross-legged trying to make yourself stop thinking. Certainly, watching a sunset or sitting by a stream or the ocean are obvious natural meditations. Watching the clouds move through the sky. Witnessing a bird fly by. Or simply quieting your mind and hearing the sound that are sounding around you. It is all meditation.

Currently, I have this small Christmas tree set up on top of my bookshelf next to one of my many statues of the Buddha. I have to keep it up high so my cat doesn't get busy with it. It's just a small fake tree that I got somewhere, some years ago. I would never cut down a tree, killing it, simply for Christmas symbolism. That's just wrong! But, this year, for some reason, the lights on that tree just seem to be exactly in the right place. The image of that tree at night, really draws me in. I sit there staring at it. It's a meditation. And, that's the thing, anything can be your meditation. You just have to see it as such.

This goes to all things life. The thing is, a lot of life is pretty mundane. A lot of your life may not be fun or make you feel good. But, if you can sit there in that traffic jam and make it your meditation, feeling the movement of some cosmic energy surrounding you, then it too can become your pathway to self-realization.

Life is what you make it. Your life is what you make it. You can make it a process of extreme emotional upheaval or you can make it a meditation, leading to a better more enlightened you. Which one do you think is better?

Interrupting Your Evolution
04/Dec/2021 06:55 AM

There is the Sanskrit word, *"Sadhana."* This term is used to describe a person's, *"Spiritual Practices."*

A person's sadhana is a personal pathway of focused evolution. It is a person choosing to enter a pathway and then become a more perfect representation of themselves by doing whatever techniques are necessary to grow mentally, physically, and spiritually. It is a personal evolution.

Sadhana is not about what someone else is doing. Sadhana is not about your admiration, your envy, or you distaste for what someone has done. Sadhana is about you focusing your energy, discovering your pathway, and then personally working to become that better you.

Most people do not practice sadhana. They do not attempt to become the better person they can be. They lock themselves in a mindset of believing that what they are is all that they can be or they set their sights on achieving what is worldly-obtainable. But, this mindset has nothing to do with psychological or spiritual growth.

Many people also place their focus outside of themselves. Some do this is the form of enhanced admiration or the worship of what some other person has achieved. Though not necessarily a bad thing, this mental focus keeps one from truly achieving what they may achieve.

The other side of this coin is, many people place their focus on other individuals in a negative fashion. Due to their own predetermined projections, they judge others by some negative method. They criticize others. But, as I have long said, if you are thinking about or speaking about anyone else, in any matter, all you are doing is shifting the focus from yourself. You are attempting to keep you or others from seeing the flaws in you and your character by calling out those you believe are harbored in someone else. Moreover, by doing this, you are providing yourself with a reason to not work on yourself and do sadhana.

Your life will ultimate be defined by what you do with your Life Time and what you become. But, what is it that you have set your sites on becoming? Do you care enough to cause yourself to enter a life pathway of spiritual evolution or do you choose to take the drug of thinking and defining who you think is good and/or who you believe is bad so you will not have to truly look at who and what you are and why you behave as you behave and do what you do?

As long as your mind is focused outside of yourself, for whatever reason, you are not focused on becoming a better version of you. You are not performing sadhana.

Most people don't. Most people do not seek to become a better internal being. Most people do not seek to correct their sins. At best, they pray or go to church to ask for forgiveness. But, how does that repair a sin? How does that cause them to become a better anything? If you want to become the better/the best you, you need to work at it. To work at it, you need to focus on what is wrong with you and what you need to improve. By placing your thoughts outside of yourself, you will never reveal the better you.

In fact, many of the so-called teachers out there, teach simply as a means to show their, *"All-Knowingness."* Though they may have learned this word or that term. Though they may have learned how to teach a certain set of techniques. Though they may be able to debate the, *"Rightness,"* of their philosophy. Though they may even hold a degree from a seminary, none of that necessarily makes them an ideal example of who they could become and/or provide them with a true reason to listen to what they have to say. In fact, the one who stands on the pulpit is more common simply locked in a state of ego and is not the one who is the true teacher.

There are many pathway to becoming a better you. But, if you do not turn off all of the outside focus and Mind Junk you will never discover the person you can truly be.

Your choice; thinking about and talking about all that is the Out There. Or, become a ray of light in a sea of darkness by become the best you that you can be. But, if you don't focus on and find a pathway of you becoming the better you that you can become, all you will be left with is that ALL that never was.

* * *

04/Dec/2021 06:55 AM

You can fill your cup until it runs over the top but that does not make your cup any more full.

The World is Full of Illusion
03/Dec/2021 07:14 AM

The world is full of illusion. I've spend much of my life delving into the reality of true reality and if what is real is actually real or is it simply an illusion.

Most people don't care. They live what they live, do what they do, and don't think about any of this too much. They could care less. They only care about what they care about. They only face the truth of life when something they care about is taken from them, when they get a terminal disease, or when someone they love dies. Then, it is face the music.

But, there is life. There is reality. There is the truth. There is truthful human interaction. Then, there is all this other stuff. All this stuff that people put out there. All the lies that people tell.

Think about the On-Line, it is so full of illusion. I think about all the people that friend me on Facebook. So many of them appear to be pretty girls. I accept and then I get a, *"Hi,"* in my messages. But, who are they really? What are they really? And, why did they friend me? What do they really want? And, if you want to start a conversation, I am happy to communicate with anyone—anyone that is real, but you have to start that conversation with more than, *"Hi."*

It's kind of like the people who are trolling for followers on Instagram. I noticed this a long time ago. People will follow you. You follow them back. Then, they stop following you. All so they can make their numbers grow, while following few. But, why? What does that prove? Me, if you're real, I'm happy to follow back—see what you post, as long as it is cool and positive. But, it has become so hard to know. So, I rarely follow back anymore. I just do not want to play that game.

Again, I'm happy to be your friend. But, why do you want to be mine?

And, that's the thing, the real world is rarely the on-line world. The on-line world is all about the illusion. It is all about the deception.

In life, you really need to constantly ask yourself, what is real? What is real with you? Are you/do you tell the truth? What false reality do you put out there? And, why? What is real with the people you know? Is what they say and do, real and true, or do they project a lie? And, why?

If you live a lie, if you project a lie, all of your reality is defined by a lie. How could you expect to experience anything else? So, if you want to live the truth, if you want to know the truth, you have to be the truth. You have to be it in your All and your Everything. If not, all you will contribute to, all you will live, is a further perpetuation of the lie.

Promises Made to a Dying Man
01/Dec/2021 05:50 PM

When Donald G. Jackson was on his deathbed at U.C.L.A. Medical Center, he was very worried about his filmmaking legacy being lost. He understood that his wife or his daughter did not possess the desire or the ability to keep his films in the public eye and his many so-called friends did not even show up to visit him in his last days. He knew I was the only one who could make it happened. I promised him I would. And, I believe I have done my best to keep his movies out there and protected. In fact, I finished a number of his unfinished films for him after he passed away.

Times change. Once up a time VHS was the ticket, then came DVD, and now we are in the world of the digital downloading—viewing via the internet on your big screen TV. I have tried to stay up with the times, keeping Don and my films out there as best as I can.

A few months back, Amazon stopped distributing DVDs from indie film companies. That action pretty much wiped out many distributors that I know. Yes, there are other DVD distribution sources out there but people don't trust them as much as Amazon. I have watched Light Source Films DVD sales plummet.

Since way back in the way back when, I released some of Don's and my films via Amazon Prime. I've tried to upload films in order to keep them available to the public. The problem is, there are a lot of restrictions via on-line sources. For example, Amazon Prime doesn't want nudity.

…Did Don ever make a film without nudity? I'm joking… Or, am I?

So, what am I to do? I have the DVDs available but, again, times are changing. Everyone wants everything online. No one is buying them.

Recently, I've started to upload some of our films to YouTube. It's not about making money as I did not do that very annoying Ad Thing on YouTube. It's about keeping Don's (and my) legacy alive and available to the public. But, there is problems...

I uploaded *Big Sister 2000* a couple of days ago. There were over ten thousand of you lucky people who got to view it. Good for you! Hope you enjoyed it. Today, YouTube took it down and told me if I ever upload anything like that again, I will be banned from YouTube and my account shut down. WOW!

Yes, there is nudity in *Big Sister 2000*. Yes, there is implied sexuality. But, there is no pornography as YouTube claims. Is *Big Sister 2000* the kind of movie that I would make? No, it was really a DGJ film. I was just behind the scenes. But, that film was in wide-release in a number of countries including the U.S. Even Amazon, with its many restrictions, distributed it on DVD. But, YouTube closed it out.

So, here I am, trying to keep my promise to a dying man alive. But, the world and the powers that be are fighting me. They don't care about Don's filmmaking legacy or about the man. What do they care about? I don't really know. Do you? I do know that there are things in play on YouTube that you or I may never understand. For example, search for *Rollergator*. You will see Rifftrax's version (who I made a deal with for them to do their bit on it). You will see reviews. But, will you see the Official Movie Release from me? Nope. You have to go to my YouTube channel page to find it. I even uploaded it twice just to see... But, the result(s) were the same. It does not come up in YouTube Search. Why?

Now, in terms of *Big Sister 2000,* I don't know... You know, there's been times when I had to do a Copyright Take Down Notice as other people have uploaded it to YouTube. Why didn't they get the serious proclamation I received? It's just weird... Really, it's just not right. But, as I learned a long-long time ago, and I have been stating for years-upon-years, *"You can only play in your own playground."* YouTube is in control of theirs, I am not.

And, like I said when he was alive and I've said since he passed-on, *"There was always a price to pay to be friends with Don."* I guess I am still paying that price.

So, what do I do now with this current set of circumstances? How do I keep Don's and my movies out in the public eye? Since all this happened, I pulled down a few of Don and my other films with nudity. I mean, if I didn't, when is YouTube going to decide they are not appropriate? So, all you people in the Out There lose out.

So, I don't know??? For all you out there, who want to support the cause and/or see the movies, I guess buy the DVD(s). You can get to them off of this website. But, other than that, I don't know where I can present the presentations while maintaining some control over their purity.

Life and the promise you make to a man on his deathbed. I keep trying! But, the powers that be in the world keep fighting me.

Representative of a Time
01/Dec/2021 02:23 PM

Today, I had the chance to look through some of my old books that I've written. I, like most authors, (I would imagine), have a collections of the books they've written in the past stuck somewhere/someplace. Me, I do too... They're all in this storage unit.

Over the past few months, I've been thinking that I should find someway to give at least some of those books away to the people that would be into them. I mean, I have some of the early chapbook editions of my early poetry and stuff like that. I've got tons of the big publisher stuff, as they sent me boxes of my books, in all kinds of languages. The martial art stuff, I gave a lot of those away, as people were always asking. But, I've stuffed a lot of the MA books away, as well. I mean, what do you do with stuff like that? Except, as I did today, look through them after years upon years of them sitting and collecting dust.

I looked at some of my early poetry books. I used to write poetry all the time. But, it seems like in all things in life, if it doesn't bring you happiness or make you money, sooner or later, those things fall away.

I could still write poetry all the time. I see the world and my life in terms of poetry. But, it just seems that I do not—at least not anymore.

Looking at that long ago written poetry, it truly provides/provided me with a look into my life. Even for me, it causes me to remember the feelings of a specific time and moment.

Looking... I think there's a few of my poetry books that are very illustrative of my life and of me in a specific era. The later stuff is all like that. But certainly, one of my later published works, *On the Hard Edge of Hollywood* is strong. Deeper back, *Scream Southeast Asia and the Dream* and *Suicide Slowly* are good, as well.

But, nobody reads poetry. At least not anymore. I always hear about these *Spoken Word* events and how people spit their truth. It seems that a lot of popular songs I hear on the radio, of late, are like that. Particularly girls, with a few guy, going on and on and on about their life, their love, and their broken hearts. That's poetry too, I guess. Just latched into a song.

How many people really want to know who a person truly is and what they have lived? I think most just want to project their own definition onto them. Even if they care enough to read their writings, do they truly want to know the inner person inside or do they simply want to define them by their own judgements and conclusions based upon what they read?

My poetry books are out there. You can read them if you want. But again, I don't think that people care about poetry anymore. Really, did they ever? Or, was it simply a trend of culture formed in the art-based reality that took hold of the world for a moment in the '50 and on into the '60s. I don't know… Some people like Buk (Bukowski) got to get rich on it. Should have been me. ☺

But, with all that/with all this, all any of us are left with is our own life. Some of us simply write about that life—telling others (in whatever abstract manner) about the who we really are and the what we really lived—feeling what we are feeling; putting those feelings into words.

What does it all mean? I don't know??? Do you? If you do, let me know. But… If I can think of someway to give out some of the book collection, I'll let you know. I'm sure there are at least a few of you out there who are truly into art—even if that art is simply presented by means of poetry.

Waste
29/Nov/2021 06:48 AM

    I tend to be up and about at weird hours of the day and of the night. I was up and out and I noticed that this truck was driving around, *"Throwing the papers,"* as it used to be called. In other words, they were delivering the newspaper. Wow… That still happens.

    I think back to this apartment I lived in a while ago. I had this very rude neighbor. It seemed everything he did really hurt my life. But, moving is expensive and not easy. Thus, I was stuck living next to him having a couple of years of my life ruined by his unconscious actions. But, anyway…

    One of the things he was responsible for, (leading to a part of this whole tale), was that he used to get the newspaper delivered. Due to the way our apartments were situated, every morning at 4:30 AM or so, BAM, a newspaper came smacking into my kitchen window waking me up. It used to be so frustrating. That is when I was first forced into thinking about the reality of the, *"Newspaper."* Then, as now, I would ponder, *"Who still get the newspaper deliver and why?"* I mean, it is so-so wasteful. …The paper that is needed to make the newspaper. …All the energy it takes to get that paper. …All the trees that are killed, if that is still how paper is made. Or, however… …All the machines that it takes to creating the paper; creating all that pollution. And then, the delivery pickup truck, out there pre-dawn throwing the paper(s). …Equaling, pollution, noise, etc., etc., etc…

    Once upon a time, in the long ago and the far-far away, I used to enjoy reading the newspaper. Every Thursday afternoon, I would head over to the Original Farmer's Market on 3rd and Fairfax, grab a latte, and sit back and read the *L.A. Weekly* as Thursdays is when it came out. On other days, when I was there or elsewhere, I may grab a copy of the *L.A. Times*. There always seemed to be so much hidden information in newspapers, if you read between the lines. But, times change. Certainly our time has changed and there is just no reason to read a physical newspaper anymore. In fact, it hurts the all and the everything if you do.

I think this is one of the big problems with life. People do what they do and that is what they do. They don't think about what their doing does to others and/or to this overall world or life space. They get lost in the what was/the what was remembered and they refuse to evolve. In that, they hurt others and other life things.

How about you? What do you refuse to change? How about you? How often do think about what your doing does to others and what it does to this place where we live our lives?

If you don't think. You are not a thinker. If you don't care, all you are is selfish. Is that what you want to be known as; a non-thinker and a selfish person?

All I can say is, think before you do, because what you do has the potential to change and/or damage someone else's everything.

* * *
29/Nov/2021 06:46 AM

We each spend about a third of our lives sleeping. When we sleep we dream. But, how many of those dreams do you remember? You spend a third of your life living in that reality but much of that reality is forgotten the moment you wake up. What happens to all that life lived and all of those memories? What do they mean and why was that reality lived if all it is becomes forgotten?

* * *

28/Nov/2021 06:34 AM

You can't buy something that isn't for sale.

A Dream Within a Dream Within a Dream
27/Nov/2021 06:52 AM

I was asleep having a dream. In that dream I woke up into another dream. I was telling a person in that second dream that I was dreaming about them in my other dream. Interesting, I had a dream about having a dream. I don't think that has ever happened before.

In Sanskrit, the term for dream is, *"Savpna."* The word for dreaming is, *"Savpana,"* But, the word that describes the fact that life is a dream, an untrue reality is, *"Dirghasvapna."*

From the Hindu perspective of consciousness, and in fact other Eastern spiritual traditions such as Buddhism, it is taught that life is a dream. It is an unreal reality that is simply a projection of the thinking mind.

Let's look at this concept for a moment. Think about your life. First of all, how much control do you really have over it? Yes, you make your own decisions based upon your set of predetermined presented choices. But, what control do you really have over reality? Do you control the weather? Can you control acts of god like earthquakes? Can you even control the actions of others with an level of absolute power? The answer to all of these questions is, no. You have, at best, minimal control over any of them and all of those other Life Things.

This is the definition of reality. This is the definition of your reality. Yet, people hold fast to the concept that they are in control when they are anything but.

To take this study a little bit deeper… What defines your reality? Is it not defined by what you believe?

There is all this stuff going on Out There. Yet, each person places their own interpretations, characterizations, and explanations onto these phenomena. Go to any church of any religion and there will be people in attendance seeking answers to their life questions and there will be someone there providing them. But, who is that all-knowing person and do they really know the Absolute Truth of anything or are they simply the one with the most highly developed ego believing that they know things that others do not?

What this tells us is that each person's reality is different. As it is different, there is no one reality that defines us all.

In the Western traditions of spirituality, all things are very cut and dry. There is right and there is wrong, there is good and there is bad. These factors are defined by individual religions and secularized sects within that religion. From this, people are taught the definition of reality that they are supposed to accept. But, there is no one universal truth. So, is what one religion or one person saying the actual truth or is it simply their interpretations of reality that others have come to and/or are supposed believe?

What this leaves us with is the Dream. The projection of what our mind envisions broadcast onto the reality of the reality that we are forced to interpret.

You live where you live. I live where I live. You do what you do. I do what I do. You believe what you believe. I believe what I believe. And, though we may try to share our beliefs and understandings with one another, your world can never be my world, just as my world can never be your world. What does this leave us with? A dream we each are living, defined in our own mind. A dream that we attempt to tell someone else about by stating, *"You were in my dream."* Then, you wake up.

* * *
26/Nov/2021 06:24 AM

If you sit anywhere for long enough everything will happen around you.

* * *

25/Nov/2021 05:57 AM

If you give them what they want they'll like you for giving it to them until they don't want it anymore.

If you don't give them what they want they'll hate you for not giving it to them because they never had the chance to find out that they don't want it anymore.

Photo Not Worth the Taking
24/Nov/2021 05:58 AM

I was up on the top level of the Eiffel Tower last week. I go to Paris periodically. I truly like the city. If all of the Persians would just stop smoking everywhere, it would be a great place. I guess no one gave them the memo about just how bad smoking is for the all and the everything of everybody.

Anyway… Though I go to Paris periodically, I don't think I've been up on the Eiffel Towel since like maybe '83. Just too touristy. But, I was up there…

This couple walked up to me and asked me to take a photo of them with this very cheap, old-school, yellow plastic film camera. You know one of those with the cheap plastic lenses. As I always do in those situations, I passed the photo duties over to my lady. I mean, hey, she has a BFA in photography and if I took the photograph, I would have to charge them a lot of money as it would be a Scott Shaw. ☺

The point being, and something my lady and I immediately discussed post the photo taking is, why would anyone use a camera like that? In this day and age, when everyone has at least a good camera in their phone, if not a great one, why go back and visit the past, (where there were fewer options for the financially challenged), in order to just get and come away with a crappy photograph?

I've seen this a lot over the past decade or so. I mean, once upon a time, when DVD technology came along, people could not get rid of their VCRs fast enough. Then came the minor resurgence of the VHS. People contact me all the time asking me if I have any of my Zen Films on video tape. Yes, video tape has a look, but is it better? My answer is, no.

This is the same when there was the cassette resurgence. And the vinyl resurgence, which has waned, but is still going on. Is it different? Yes. Is it better? No.

For some reason, people look to this past with some weird sort of envy. They wish they were there. Certainly, eras like the 60s and the 80s draw up all kinds of worshipers. But, what is depicted on the silver screen or in photographs is not what was actually lived. I won't go into all of that but just take my word for it. If you were there, great. If not, don't fantasy about it. It wasn't all that it was cracked up to be.

So, what does this tell us? It tells us: things change, times change. Technology makes things better. Yeah, you can look to the past if you want to. Yeah, you can still find a cheap crappy camera if you want to embrace the past. But, why? Ten years down the road do you want to look at a photograph where you can actually make out the faces and the scenery or do you want to look at a faded-out blur of that time and that place that can never be lived again?

* * *
24/Nov/2021 05:09 AM

You can't get what you want if you don't know what you want.

If you do know what you want that does not mean that you can get it.

*   *   *
23/Nov/2021 03:03 PM

If you didn't know then you wouldn't know.

Sometimes you need to pretend that you don't know.

Excuses
22/Nov/2021 07:28 AM

    I always find life very interesting. I always find the excuses people make very interesting. Do you ever listen to a person making an excuse? What goes on is that they have done something wrong, inadequate, or something that you did not like, appreciate, or something that hurt you, and then, based upon what you said, they dig up some justification and/or rationalization for what they have done in an attempt to rationalize their actions. If you tell them, that is not good enough or you call them out for what they are saying then things can turn into an argument. But, the fact of the fact is, if someone is making an excuse, that is all they are doing. They are not saying that they are sorry. They are not attempting to remedy the situation. Nor are they trying to repair any damage that they created.

    The next time you hear someone making an excuse, think about it. The next time you make an excuse think about what you are saying and why.

Biography
22/Nov/2021 06:52 AM

There used to be a lot of hits on the Biography and FAQ pages of my website. Now, that has greatly diminished. I guess everyone knows who and what I am. Or, maybe they just no longer care. That might be the best thing.

A lot of people used to talk shit about me on the various posting sites on the internet. Some even did elaborate presentations. But, of all of those people who talked the shit, not one of them had or has ever met me. So, how can/could they know anything about me? Just trolls or people that wanted to make a name for themselves by using my name. Though some of those things are still up and out there, that kind of stuff has also diminished. Again, maybe people just no longer care. AOK with me. What I do is what I do…

Magazines and newspapers used to ask to interview me all the time. Do those things even exist anymore?

My entire life has been lived and defined by the abstract and the alternative. The stories I could tell you… But, even in the stories I have already told you, nothing about my existence was ever normal. Some may view that as good or artistic or something??? Me… I don't know… Living like that/this is not easy.

My school years were nuts—living where and how I did. My high school, I went to the <u>then</u> very progressive Alternative School of Hollywood High School. It was much more set up and structured like the graduate division of a University than a high school. That was a good things; I guess? As my life by that point was so nothing about high school that if I had not attended a school set up in that fashion I, most highly, would not have graduated; which would not have been a good thing. Then, I would not have been able to go to college. …Which/where post by B.A. and my first stint in Grad School was also structured in and by the Alternative.

I avoided traditional schools. Good or bad, that was my younger years.

My art: martial and otherwise was also abstract. Though my martial arts training was based in the traditional—for years upon years upon years. But, I saw the flaws in all that. Being at the center point of martial arts evolution in its early(er) years in the U.S., I saw a lot of the shortcomings of organizational structure—something that if you were not there, you could never understand. There was and still is a lot of bullshit that went on and goes on. It truly makes one ponder that if there were no rank and/or school, style, or organizational pride polluting the systems of self-defense how much better the all and the everything of the martial arts could be.

Art: painting, film, music, writing, and otherwise, forget about it… If you don't get it you will never get it. You just can't force people to understand art.

The reason I'm saying all this is, look to yourself—look to your own life… Where do you find yourself in the spectrum of reality? Where do you find yourself within the boundaries of normal? What created who and what you are and why?

Many people look outside of themselves. They don't want to look within. They want to place their focus outside of themselves. With this, they do not have to take a look at who and what they truly are. This is why sports are so popular. This is why Reality TV is so popular. This is why sites like TMZ thrive. People want to take the drug of OUTSIDE.

How about you? Who are you? Truly, who are you? Do you know? Are you honest with yourself? Are you truthful with yourself about why you do what you do? Do you ever even ponder any of this?

Life… Your life is wholly defined by your existence. Your existence is defined by what you choose to do with your time. What are you doing with your time? How is what you are doing with your time affecting you, your life, and you're legacy? And, how is it affecting the anyone, the everyone else?

    If you don't take the time to study this… If you don't take the time to question, study, and view how the outside world sees you and why… If you don't take the time to know who you are and why you are… If you don't contemplate the YOU that the world has created and the YOU that YOU have created, then what will your life have actually meant?

    If you don't know the definition of you, how can anyone else know the definition of you?

The Exhibition of Power
21/Nov/2021 05:37 AM

    I just finished watching the new Netflix series, *Tiger King 2*. Though not as bizarrely interesting as the first one, what this edition to the series did was to truly portray how some/certain individuals exercise their power over other creatures, (like animals) to supplement their own gains. Whither these own gains be money, control, sex, claimed American Rights, fulfilling their own interpersonal lack of selfhood, or whatever. But, no matter how you slice it, there are some people out there who do some very-very bad things to animals and to people so that they can get their fix of power and of control.

    If you look around life, you see this all the time. People <u>do</u> things and <u>say</u> things and create situations so that they can unleash their power. They do things to maintain power over others. But, why do they do this? In all cases it is done to fulfill that LOSS, that emotionlessness, that not-enoughness that dwells within them.

    This problem is rooted in the fact that some people do not have the developed Self Awareness or possess the ability to be able to truly see themselves. They do not hold the ability to be able to truly look within themselves and find out who and what they truly are and pinpoint their lackings. As they do not possess this ability, they do all kinds of BAD things that hurt other living creature: (animal, human, and otherwise), and in fact, by behaving in this manner, they do things that hurt ALL LIFE.

    I once had a friend who breed Rottweilers. It was just appalling. He had these beautiful dogs and they were beat into submission by this leather belt he had hanging near their small fenced-in enclosure where they were forced to live. I would just shiver in disbelief when he would proudly beat them into doing whatever it is he wanted. He had this one very-very large, (probably the biggest Rottweiler I had ever seen), animal and the dog was so messed up from being beaten all the time that when he was happy and being petted he would growl. He did this because that was the only emotion he knew. Whenever a pup was born with some white in it, (as I guess that is bad in the Rottweiler breed), the guy would kill that puppy. How horrible! How selfish! How unaware! How life WRONG! But, that guy is still alive. The dogs are not. Thankfully he no longer breeds dogs. This is just one example of the heartless exhibition of power and control that goes on all the time and you could see a lot of it in *Tiger King 2*.

If we look at life, people extend this behavior of their exhibition of power to all elements of their life. They do it with animals, they do it with things, they (especially) do it with people. They do it, but they are so unaware as to their own inner emotions, the own inner demons, and their own inner motivations that they cannot stop. They simply find new and ever-evolving justifications and excuses for their actions.

I think in this period of history, (where we find currently find ourselves), during the age of the pandemic, during the #woke and #cancelculture, we are all bombarded by people doing all kinds of self-motivated actions; all initiated by a misguided sense of Self. So much so that many individuals believe that they have the right to exhibit and project their own personal beliefs onto others. But, do they? My feeling is, if you hurt anyone or anything for any reason, then what you are doing is wrong. But, who owns that? Who owns what they do? Who studies themselves to the degree that they can view, weed out, and learn how to control and heal those dark places inside themselves where a person's personal quest for power hurts others? Very few.

So, what happens when we see this type of behavior? What can we do? What happens when we notice it in ourselves? The answer is we (personally) must be strong enough to correct it. This does not mean confronting that someone else who is doing it, as all that leads to is confrontation based on personal bias. But, it all comes down to the YOU. The YOU who is aware and enlightened enough to be able to stop yourself from doing bad things to other people's life—all life, and this Life Space in general. It must be YOU who corrects any pain, hurt, or damage you have created. It must be YOU who seek out the lacking in yourself and never-never allows that deficiency to cause you seek out power over others (by any means) which only leads to the instigation of pain. And, NEVER NEVER make excuses for your desire for power over others. STOP IT! FIX IT! Be more than someone who's desire for power hurts the life of someone, something, or anything.

Buying into the Illusion
20/Nov/2021 06:01 AM

Ever since the dawning of the age of the internet it has been very easy to witness the hold that illusion has over people. Once upon a time, in the long ago and the far-far away, you had to know someone to watch them fall prey to the promise of what was never to be. But, then came the world wide web and certain people immediately found a way to give and to gain and to believe that what is in front of their eyes may actually be theirs.

I think back to the early stages of the internet—before that was even its name. I was writing my dissertation and I discovered that I could access certain newspapers and certain books on my computer. It wasn't even known as being on-line yet. But, it was a great boon as I was able to get information and I did not even have to travel to and go digging through microfiche at local libraries.

But, then too, I saw people wasting all kinds of time doing what latter became, *"Chatting,"* on what were best described as, *"Posting boards."*

People would claim a screen name. The screen names weren't permanent back then. They changed every time you phoned-in and listened to the dial-up tone. You hoped you could your same name. But, sometimes someone beat you to it.

But, what did all that type-talking mean? What did it equal? What does it equal? All it does it kill your time—take your Life Time and what are you left with? Words forgotten that meant very little.

Then things started to improve. With visuals it all changed. People could see what they thought they saw. But, was any of it real?

Not that long ago, maybe a couple of decades, sites like Amazon begin to offer their clientele their own pages where people could post their wish list. I remember whenever a pretty girl's birthday was coming up, they would reminded all the people out their who followed them, by whatever means was possible (back then), to buy them what was on that list. Like a Wedding Registry men bowed down and paid out. But, who did they pay out to? The fact is, it was only a fantasy. A fantasy they would never personally know.

What all this drove was the illusion of the illusion. The promise of what could never be.

Think about it, maybe think about yourself, what have you fallen under the spell of the illusion about? Who have you fallen under the spell of their illusion to? Who have you tried to make fall under your illusion? And, what was the basis of any of this?

People rarely study their inner-emotions. They just randomly think. They simply impulsively act. They do what they do without any consciousness as to why they are doing. They just want. When they are presented with the possibility of the illusion then they become lost from all reason and they do with no true sense of why they are doing.

Truly ponder this for a moment… How much of what you do is done on the basis of illusion? How much of what you do is based in fantasy? How much of what you do is based upon the desired hope of getting that whatever or whomever it is that you are dreaming about?

Think to your life… How many of those illusions that you have fallen prey to did you actually live?

Now, turn this around, how much of your life is based upon presenting an illusion? How much false hope do you put out there with the intention of getting that gift that you want on your Amazon wish list? And, do you care about what that promised illusion is doing to that other person?

Life is an interactive process. Once upon a time, it was primarily based upon one-on-one. At least at that stage of human history, illusion was more interactive. But now, all that is lost. All there is has become the image of the Out

There. But, what is the Truth in that Out There? Moreover, why do you let it control you? The answer to that question is because you do not have a Conscience Control of Self. You do not have a Focused Principal of Life. Due to this fact, you will give to what you can never have. You will do things for those you will never truly know. You may believe the illusion. You may believe the promise. You may follow the lies that they speak. But, as you can never live a true reality with them (with that) all you are doing is casting your life to an existence of being wholly defined by falsity and illusion.

Since the dawning of rising human consciousness, spiritual teachings have warned that all life is illusion. That one must protect themselves from falling prey to that illusion. But, do you? Do you walk the path of illusion-filled worship? Do you walk the path of illusion-filled portrayal? In either case, all you are doing is walking a road to No Self Awareness. If you do this—if you follow this path, what will your life have meant in its final portrayal?

Out a' Control
19/Nov/2021 03:59 AM

To tell the story... There is this sweet young lady who had taken a couple of my courses on filmmaking—we had communicated a lot about filmmaking and she was set to go up on her first full-length feature. She invited me to come and watch her film this project and I was impressed, it was all so Zen (Zen Filmmaking) and free flowing. She totally got it. Like she said to me on the set, *"Just like you said, Scott, I'm grabbing the shadows and the energy."*

Maybe a week later, I go back to her set. The change was scary. She had a couple of young female child actors, several crew members and she was doing the same shot over and over—time after time after time. Totally non-Zen Filmmaking style. It was really shocking to witness the difference just a few days had made. She was throwing orders, trying to get the kids to do the scene exactly the way she (the director) saw it in her mind. It was going on and on and on and on.

They took a break. A break she obviously didn't want to take. She was hyped. I walked over to her, to kind of give her some friendly advice—to hopefully push her back in the right direction, if you will. But, all she wanted to do was kiss me. Maybe better put, make out with me. She even suggested that we go somewhere private where she could have her way with me. Wow! Now, as agreeable as I normally would have been to any of those suggestions, I could tell she was just running on pure adrenaline and I would have just become another part of the drug regimen she was currently ingesting. I mean, she was on! So, I said thanks but no thanks. I went my way that day. She continued to film. ...Though I cannot truly say that I wished that I had not taken her up on her offer.

It's been a couple of months now and though we spoke during that time frame, I never did a real sit down with her until now. What went on is that she lost it. She got all obsessional crazy about her film. She spent all her money trying to make it the way she wanted; spending on cast, and crew, and locations. When her money was gone she hit up her credit cards and, I guess, even got a couple of new ones; which she maxed out. Now, the movie is still not complete and she had to go and get some crappy job she really hates just to stay a float.

Whenever I see or hear about situations like these, it reminds me of this great song by one of the seminal bands that helped to orchestrate the Paisley Underground era of L.A. music in the '80, *The Three O'clock* and their song, *"Wild,"* with the central lyric, *"When I go wild."* Though the lyrical subject matter of that song is a bit different, the title alone, describes what so many people have the potential to do in and with their life if they allow themselves to be unchecked—if they lose control.

You know, at the root of *Zen Filmmaking* is freedom. It's about no structure. It's about taking hold of the moment and seizing it. ...Tuning into it and expressing its perfection. Allowing all things to be as all things are—not attempting to control them but becoming a part of them and utilizing them as an expression of your art.

Now, take this to the level of All Life. Think how much better your life would be/could be if you just followed the pathway of what is. ...If you did not try to take control over it and try to force it to your whims.

Think of all of the life complications you have found yourself encountering as you have passed through your life; weren't they all created by you trying to take and/or maintain control? Most probably were. But, if all you do is let life be... If all you do is exist within it's perfection... If all you do is not try to control what you really can't really control then doesn't everything just become that much simpler?

As for my filmmaking friend, I have watched this process in so many people—so many indie filmmakers who lose their path and their project, and, in some cases, their financial standing due to trying to crate and film the perfection that exists in their mind but can never be brought to life. I've also seen this in the life-actions of people who are doing nothing more than trying to live their life the way they wanted it to be live—the life they see in their mind but cannot bring to reality.

So, think about this the next time you have that Mind Vision that you wish to make a reality. Is the reality that is your reality really that much worse than that movie projecting on the image screen of your mind? And, what will it do to your film project, your life movie, your life reality, if you chase that mental vision and fail? Then what are you left with? Will all you be left with is no completed movie and maybe a lot of life debt?

THE
ZEN

www.ingramcontent.com/pod-product-compliance
Lightning Source LLC
Chambersburg PA
CBHW070736170426
43200CB00007B/544